Be *Weirdly* Wonderful!

Embrace your Differences

Five practical ways to lead your best life

Also by Jenny Woolsey

Ride High Pineapple
Brockwell the Brave
Land of Britannica
Daniel Barker: By Power or Blight
Daniel Barker: Journey to Egypt
Amy and Phoenix
Amy and Phoenix: Time to Shine
Simon Sees

Be *Weirdly* Wonderful!

Embrace your Differences

Five practical ways to lead your best life

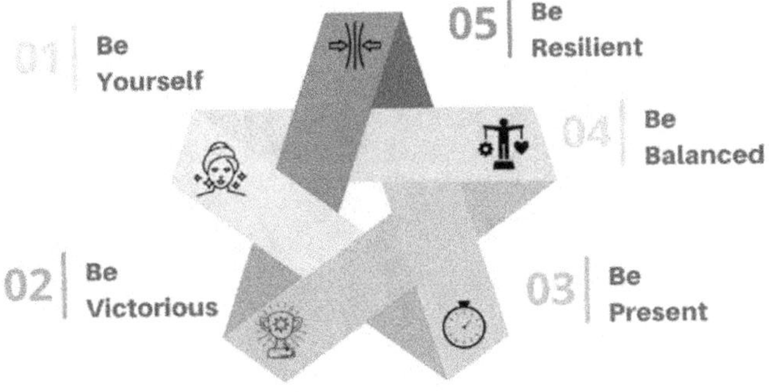

Jenny Woolsey

Published by Pearls of Wisdom Press 2024

A catalogue record for this book is available from the National Library of Australia.
Book cover design services by
htttp://selfpublishinglab.com/
http://www.jennywoolsey.com/
ISBN:
978-0-6488337-6-5 (pbk)
978-0-6488337-7-2 (e-bk)

To Ken with all my love

Contents

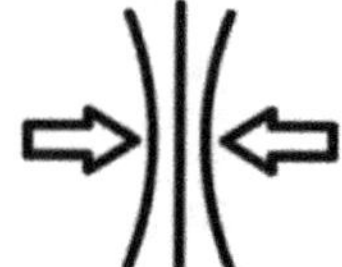

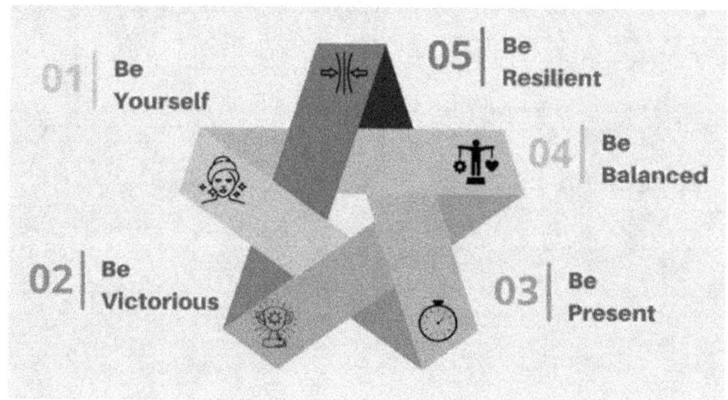

01 | Be Yourself
05 | Be Resilient
04 | Be Balanced
02 | Be Victorious
03 | Be Present

Author's Preface

'Googly eyes. You've got googly eyes,' the gang of boys chanted at the girl as she scurried past them. She tried to ignore their hurtful barbs, intent on her destination. For her, this was a daily occurrence. The triangular-roofed brick building with the sign stating 'Library' was straight ahead down the covered walkway. Beyond those tinted glass doors, nestled on wooden shelves and with brightly-coloured spines, sat stories with magical places, mythical characters and, most importantly, people who weren't bullied for how they looked. This girl with the honey-blonde hair spent hours engrossed in those wonderful worlds—far away from the cruelty of her existence.

Every human is unique but if we're too different and we deviate too far from the 'norm', society often deems us as unacceptable. And the consequences of being placed in the 'unacceptable' box can be traumatically severe with bullying, rejection, exclusion and isolation, and being made to feel inferior and worthless.

In the opening scene, the girl with the prominent bulgy eyes and who found comfort in reading, received the daily sting of society's unacceptance. Who do you think this girl was? Yes, she was *me*.

Welcome to *Be Weirdly Wonderful! Embrace your differences.* In this preface, I would like to introduce myself and explain my motivation for writing this wonderful book.

I'm Jenny Woolsey, an international author and speaker and a retired primary school teacher who loves to write, create pottery and advocate for people living with disability. My vision is impaired and I'm challenged by anxiety and depression. I'm also a single mum of three and the carer for my youngest. Born in the 1960s, I was the first in my lineage to be diagnosed with a rare craniofacial syndrome—a condition causing facial and skull deformities. The diagnosis soon after birth was *Crouzon syndrome*, initially called 'Crouzon Disease'. My face was very different from a so-called 'normal' baby and, as you could well imagine, I was a massive shock to my family.

Two decisions that my parents made influenced my entire life. First, they took me home from the hospital. In the 1960s, there was an option to leave the baby in an adoption ward or send them to an institution. Historical records on institutions reveal how horrific they were. I shudder at the thought. My parents also envisioned a life for me that mirrored my older brothers'—a vision and decision actioned the moment I came home. These two decisions challenged the common attitudes of the day when people hid children away who were 'deformed' or 'different.'

I am thankful to my parents for making these pioneering choices for me as my childhood was rich in experiences, exploration, fun, laughter and self-discovery. Pushback, though, came from people in the community who didn't like the look of me and, from birth, I endured verbal and physical bullying, pointing, stares, rejection and discrimination. Growing up was hard but my loving and protective family and friends supported me.

Unlike many authors who write a personal development book, I haven't experienced one specific, life-changing event. Instead, my life has been a lifetime of hardships and a rollercoaster of struggles and challenges, sprinkled with fairy dust in the good times and in the moments of wonder and joy. I've made successful and poor life choices and lived with the consequences of these. I've failed and I've achieved. I've hit rock bottom with my mental health and learnt how to manage it. I've loved and then left because of domestic violence. I've miscarried babies and raised three children who needed extensive help (on my own since 2020). I've rejected and then returned to my Christian faith. And I've lost and then found my identity.

Despite what life has dealt me, I stand before you a woman who is self-assured, independent and has learnt to find happiness amid storms. The book cover photo was taken on a whim whilst holidaying in Sydney. I was really sick at the time but was desperate to see an ancient Egyptian exhibition that fitted with my middle grade, Daniel Barker series. My partner and I were driving around sightseeing and the rainbow appeared. We jumped out of the car and I positioned my hand. Ken snapped the picture, and we raced back just as the storm hit. I wanted this photo, with my au natural face and clothes on the cover, as it epitomises my attitude towards life.

I have embraced who I am and I'm leading my best life.

Be Weirdly Wonderful! Embrace your differences focuses on five areas of personal development and contains practical research-based strategies and mindsets that have helped me, combined with illustrations from my life. The book is divided into five chapters: Be Yourself, Be Victorious, Be Present, Be Balanced and Be Resilient.

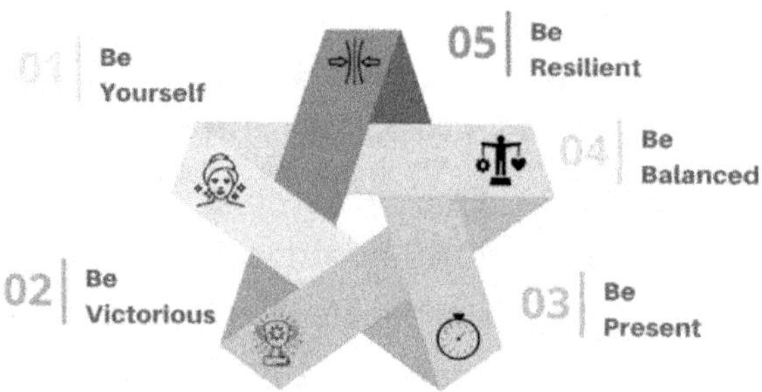

Regardless of your background or life experiences, *Be Weirdly Wonderful! Embrace your differences* aims to empower you, boost your self-confidence, help you to embrace your true self and guide you towards leading your best life. This book is written from my heart and is for you.

God bless,

Jenny Woolsey
Author, Speaker, Potter, Disability Advocate
M.Ed(Hons)
www.jennywoolsey.com

Chapter 1 - *Introduction*

Before I jump into the main part of the book where I explain my five practical strategies, I would like to expand on my life story.

As I mentioned in the preface, I was born in the 1960s in Brisbane, Australia, with a rare craniofacial condition called Crouzon syndrome. *Craniofacial* means 'affecting the formation of the skull and facial bones'. When I was born, the statistic for having Crouzons was 1 in 250,000. It is now 1 in 100,000. If I was a diamond, I'd have been worth a fortune but, alas, I wasn't! The change in the gene FGFR2 Fibroblast Growth Factor Receptor 2 affects the proteins that construct the skull and facial bones, causing stunted growth.

I was born with a moderate form of the syndrome and have most of the classic characteristics. To describe in a simple way how I looked, I would say the following: My skull bones were fused prematurely with no soft spots (known as *craniosynostosis*), I had shallow eye sockets with bulgy eyes, a curved small nose, flat cheekbones and midface, a small receded upper jaw with a high arched palate, low set ears and a larger more prominent lower jaw. I looked abnormal.

By the time I was ten months old, my parents noticed that my health was deteriorating. I often cried and wasn't reaching my developmental milestones. An x-ray, with my parents having to hold me down, showed that my brain was being compressed by my skull. I would have had a massive headache! In fact, the pressure was so great that my brain was wearing holes in the bones.

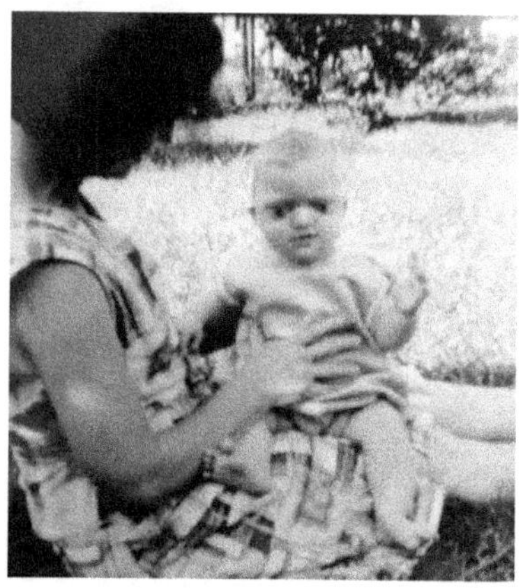

Nana holding me. Circa nine months

My family doctor contacted the pioneering neurosurgeon, Doctor Kenneth Grant Jamieson (1925-1976), who had seen the condition before. He operated to expand my skull in two surgeries. If it wasn't for Dr Jamieson, I'd have died. Mum says that I started to pull myself up and walk afterward.

To some adults in society, particularly those with the 'freak show' mentality, my uniqueness meant I didn't belong and I should either be kept hidden at home in a cupboard or put in an institution. To many of the kids at school and outside of school, I was an oddity and a target.

My mother often recalls the occasion when she took my brothers and me to see The Magic Pudding puppet show. I was only two or three years old at the time. Mum dressed me in my Sunday finest, a lemon dress with pretty ribbons, and I clasped a blue handbag especially crocheted for me by my grandmother. After the show, people milled around in the foyer. One of those was a photographer taking family portraits for sale. My parents' camera had accidentally been dropped in the surf so they were without one and Mum saw this as the perfect opportunity to get a photo of us three kids. She approached the photographer and requested a photo. He looked at me and turned his back on her. Mum followed him and asked again. He looked at me and this time actually refused. Mum, incensed, demanded he take a photo. The photographer sighed, turned towards us and snapped. There was no posing and no 'say cheese' like the other children received. Nothing. That was how society generally saw me. I was a nothing.

The photo taken at The Magic Pudding puppet show

It wouldn't have taken long for me, as an intelligent child, to pick up on what society was telling me. And consequently, as a youngster, a teen and then a young adult, I expended a lot of energy trying to prove to the world that I was a valuable human being. I wasn't just a face. Behind that face was

Jenny—an intelligent girl with feelings, a personality, gifts and talents. A girl with dreams.

As I mentioned in the preface, my parents wanted me to have the same life and opportunities that my brothers would have. They took me out and about and sometimes even pushed me unwillingly forward into society. I learnt to swim and to play tennis, the organ and guitar. I joined Brownies, went through the Girl Guide movement and participated in all school activities and extra-curricular ones. I also enjoyed going to birthday parties and sleepovers at a friend's house— doing what most children do. My parents wanted me to be leading my best life.

School was a complex environment. I loved learning and being involved in the band, choir, library and sports teams. And I loved my friends. But school meant daily bullying, name calling, being pushed over, being left out, picked last and more. Every day, a dagger was thrust into my heart. 'Sticks and stones may break my bones but names will never hurt me,' that popular nursery rhyme which I would frequently chant, is a LIE. A huge lie.

It was only a few years ago, upon reconnecting with a school friend, that she told me about an incident in primary school which I have no recollection of. At the time, I was being bullied by a group of boys and she punched the main offender. She was sent to the principal's office in serious trouble. After school, she explained the incident to her parents. Furious, her parents stormed up to the school seeking a meeting with the principal. Her parents were angry their daughter was in trouble for standing up for me and they demanded that the school stop the kids from picking on me.

But the principal didn't intervene or punish the bullies and the kids continued.

Being born with such a rare syndrome meant I didn't know anyone like me. And when I visited my paediatrician, Dr Grantley Stable, I frequently felt like a circus exhibit. He would show me off to student doctors and I hated it. I recall, with a shudder, sitting on the clinician's patient bed surrounded by a mob of curious faces talking about me, not to me. It was traumatic.

Apart from having my skull expanded, no other surgeries were performed in Australia until 1975 in Adelaide, South Australia, and 1977 in Brisbane, Queensland. Obviously, the lack of specialist facial plastic surgeons in the country didn't just affect me. Any person born with a congenital or acquired facial difference couldn't be helped unless they could afford to visit Paris. Why Paris? Because, in Paris, Dr Paul Tessier (1917-2008), considered the father of modern craniofacial surgery, was performing groundbreaking innovative techniques to rebuild faces.

Kindergarten photo day

In 1977, a craniofacial unit opened in Brisbane with Dr Anthony Emmett (plastic surgeon) and Dr Leigh Atkinson (neurosurgeon). I was the second patient operated on, after Robert Hoge who received all the publicity, but the first child with Crouzon syndrome.

The ten-hour surgery involved a complete facial reconstruction. Sections of my ribs and hip bone were used to rebuild parts of my face and my jaws were cut, repositioned, and realigned.

Unfortunately, like all surgeries but particularly in pioneering ones, there were enormous risks involved. My ophthalmologist, Dr Harold 'Paul' Spiro (1926-2022), advised my parents against having the surgery as blindness could result but, in love and wanting me to have a better life as well as better health (for my eyes to close and improved breathing), they decided to go ahead with it.

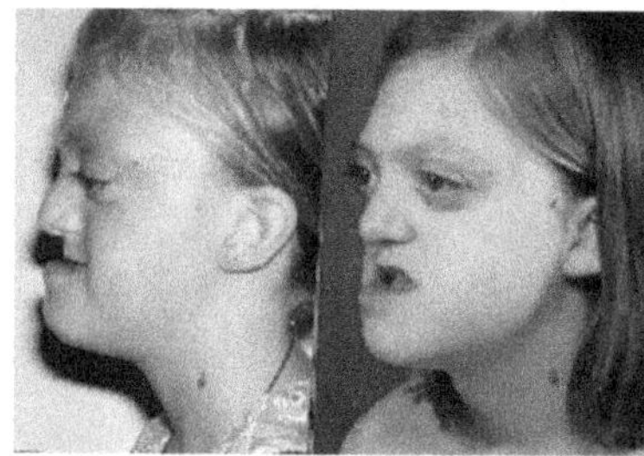
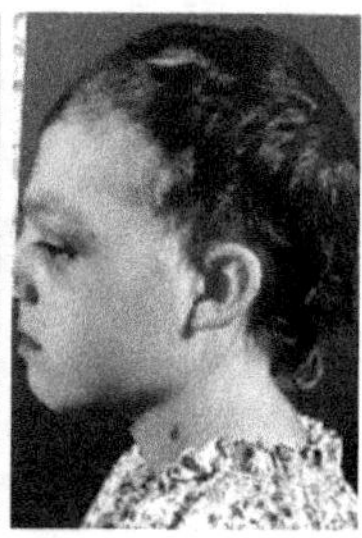

Pre-surgery and post-surgery (photos courtesy of Dr Emmett)

Unfortunately, Dr Spiro's fear came true. Severe optic nerve swelling, known as atrophy, caused me to lose the majority of sight in my left eye. The eye muscles were stretched, causing a turn in the eye and misalignment of my eyes. My right eye was also affected by a major loss of peripheral vision. After the surgery, I retained only 30 degrees of my visual field on the right side of my right eye (called *Hemianopia*). I wore glasses for short-sightedness before the surgery but, afterwards, I was more significantly impaired and needed vision aids to help me ... and would never be able to drive.

The surgery was a medical success in improving my breathing, my eyes could now fully close and my jaws were aligned. The surgery was also a social and emotional success.

The dramatic transformation of my face generally allowed me a sabbatical from the stares and being made fun of. I did say 'generally' … as I thought the boys in my class who had teased me, would stop when I went back to school. But no, they continued to taunt me about the wig I wore that covered my bald, multi-scarred head.

A year post-surgery circa eleven years old

As the saying goes, all good things must come to an end and, within a couple of years, my face began to change and regress. My midface bones stayed where they were surgically moved to. But my lower jaw continued to grow, meaning my top jaw was soon back behind my lower and my eyes became bulgy again.

The bullying began on my first day of high school.

With distress, I watched my lovely 'new face' disappear as my adult face grew. It's hard enough being a teenager with self-identity questions, the existential crises, the emotional rollercoaster and the rest, without such a significant visible difference. I deeply yearned to blend back in. I hated standing out everywhere I went and trying to prove myself to the world. I hated being rejected and people thinking I was intellectually disabled. I hated that I was becoming a perfectionist. I hated the staring, the pointing, the name calling—I wasn't the Elephant Man or Frankenstein!

I was driven by my need to prove myself as a valuable and intelligent human being and this was a daily affair.

Circa fifteen years old

In high school, I involved myself in as many activities as I could and aimed for the highest marks I could get. My self-esteem was linked to my achievements—School Debating Team, Champion Speller, Queensland Day Essay Writing Competition winner, winning ribbons at the local show for my schoolwork, Queen's Guide Award, being Honoured Queen of Job's Daughters and more.

With perfectionism and outward signs of achievement being my constant companion, failure severely wounded me and I learnt to avoid things that led to it. I also developed two personalities. I was the loud extrovert around my friends and family and a shy introvert with acute social anxiety around strangers. Out in public, I'd walk with my head down or wear sunglasses so no one could see my eyes. I got tired of wolf-whistles from the back and then rude jeering from the front.

At seventeen years old, my plastic surgeon informed me that I could have another surgery if I wanted it. It would be a similar surgery to the one in 1977. My desperation to fit into society overtook the fear I had of going under the knife and the painful and hard recovery process.

I can't put into words how strong the need was for me to be a stock-standard Homo sapien.

Towards the end of 1985, aged eighteen, I underwent the second horrific reconstruction with more rib bone grafts and more moving and wiring of the jaws. More pain. More swelling. More vision loss…

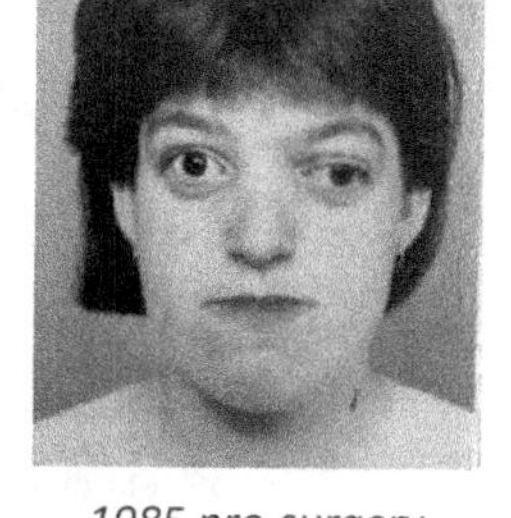

1985 pre-surgery (photo courtesy of Dr Emmett)

Was it worth it?

Euphorically, yes! Why? Because society gave me the tick of approval. I knew I had passed the 'society test' soon after the surgery when I went into Brisbane and walked down the Queen Street mall as I had done all my life. Previously, I'd been treated as a leper — stared at, pointed at, made fun of by teenagers etc. But no one took any notice of me. Can you imagine what that must have felt like?! It was as if my demon had been exorcised. For me, at that time, the torture had been worth it.

With this new acceptance, I tried to forget my childhood and the fact that I'd been born with this 'grotesque deformity' (as it was described in 1977 by the Australian Women's Weekly, the widely read national magazine, that ran a feature on the Australian Craniofacial Unit). And I was mostly successful at being able to push my childhood trauma down and could usually ignore that I'd been born with a facial difference.

Eight months post-surgery on my 19th birthday

I say 'usually ignore' because I could never fully ignore it. Medical appointments, speech therapy, my ongoing visual impairment, my still bulgy eyes but to a lesser extent than before, the turn in my left eye and the large ugly tracheostomy scar on my neck from 1977 meant there was still evidence.

Pre-surgery, I worked in an educational bookstore. Post-surgery, I moved two hours away from home to Toowoomba to study primary school teaching. Even though I'd suffered from terrible bullying at school, I'd always wanted to be a primary school teacher like my mum. Upon commencing my studies, my face was still swollen and bruised and my speech poor from my jaws being moved.

No psychological help had been offered or suggested pre- or post-surgery. It was just 'get on with life' as it had been when I was a child. And with 'just getting on with life', my low self-esteem, anxiety and the need to prove myself continued as stumbling blocks to me leading my best life.

Every year from my first teaching prac in 1986 until I retired in 2014, a child in my class would comment on my big eyes and ask me what had happened to my neck. My reply consisted of a simple explanation about being born with my eyes this way and the tracheostomy was where a tube was put in my throat so I could breathe during an operation on my face. That

Early years of teaching - 1990s

usually got an 'ewww' or a look of awe. Once the children were given an explanation, all was good—until the next year when it was repeated. My students often protected me from other children who made fun of my eyes or said I was scary looking, and they would come and tell me the mean things that were being said about me. I was a kind and caring teacher who wouldn't tolerate bullying and, in response, many of the students would draw me beautiful pictures, make me special cards, bring me flowers and tell me I was pretty. I lapped up these affirmations like a cat with cream. They went a small way to heal my childhood pain.

I think I can honestly say that, when you feel rejection deep in the marrow of your bones, stupid and regrettable decisions can be made.

Hearing 'I love you' and 'I want to be seen out in public with you as your boyfriend' was all I wanted from Year 5 onwards. I had friends who were boys and really good friends too ... but that wasn't enough for me. That wasn't enough to remove my 'you're deformed and worthless' thoughts.

I met a guy at my church's youth group within the first six months of moving to Toowoomba. He was also studying at uni as a mature-age student. He looked hot in his trendy clothes and I was smitten. I was still swollen from my surgery and he admitted that he was a bit scared of me and wondered what had happened.

He drove a car (I rode a pushbike), owned a computer (which was way better than my electric typewriter), had welcoming parents who treated me like their daughter and, like me, he loved water sports and the outdoors. To me, he was my perfect match. In my opinion, the robot Dexter on the Perfect Match dating show couldn't have matched us better.

The giant red flag flapping in front of my face like a bullfighter's cape was our constant fighting. These frequent, heated episodes were always related to him wanting his own way and me wanting mine. But I overlooked this as ... *he loved me.*

To cut a long story short, I married him after three years of dating. I did not know it but, by then, I was superglued into a cycle of abuse.

After seven years of coercive control, the 'love is blind' scales had fallen from my eyes and I wanted out. Being a Christian, though, my belief of 'until death do us part' kept me there. A sack of burgeoning depression consumed me.

We started attending a new church and I bravely voiced my concerns to the pastor who suggested marriage counselling. My husband threatened me during this time saying that, if I left, he would come after me as no one else could have me.

In the blackest hole, where I could not see a light at the end, I earnestly prayed for God to change him or to give me an escape route. As each day passed with nothing happening, I sank lower and lower and lower into that black dog. With little hope, I came to the conclusion that 'until death do us part' would be the way out—that death being my own.

I started to plan my suicide by overdose and began researching what pills would work.

During a counselling session soon after, while curled in a foetal position on the couch, the words 'Can I go home for the weekend? It's the start of the school holidays,' sprang from my lips, directed at the counsellor.

She replied, 'Yes, that would be a really good idea.'

My husband said, 'No.'

'It would be good for you both,' the counsellor said.

In the end, he reluctantly agreed.

Once inside the safety of my parents' locked front door, I burst into tears and explained the goings-on. I'd put on such a mask they were oblivious to the full extent of the abuse and my fragile state of mind.

'You're not going back to him,' my dad stated.

My childhood bedroom, with its lavender flowered wallpaper, Garfield posters, Hobbytex paintings and 'God loves you' stickers, became my sanctuary.

As you could well imagine, my husband was devastated and angry about this news and tried to win me back. His parents were upset at losing me, too. Their emotions created guilt and I was sometimes tempted to change my mind. But my dad's constant words, 'You're not going back to him. You deserve better', kept me saying, 'No.' It sure wasn't easy.

My first marriage lasted ten years and, with the dissolution of it, I turned my back on my faith. I was too embarrassed to go back to church and, I'd have to say, angry at God for letting me marry this man.

After being separated for six months, I moved out of my parents' home and lived on my own. Loneliness danced with my messed-up mental health. I couldn't drive due to my low vision and I'd lost 'his' friends and our activities/sports. Chatrooms on the Internet seemed to be the answer. I quickly became obsessed with the positive attention I received and my ravenous low self-esteem was fed.

That decision, to find out what chatrooms were like, led to bouncing straight into my next marriage just seven months after the divorce was final.

The guy who became my husband lived in the bright lights of Miami in America. Amazingly, he ticked all the boxes on my 'this is what I want in my next husband' and the 'this is what I don't want in my next husband' checklists.

Three months after meeting online, he flew out to Australia to meet me in person. My friends were concerned but I was sure everything would be fine. At the airport, I nervously waited with butterflies flapping incessantly in my stomach and holding a stuffed kangaroo. But I didn't have the 'fall into each other's arms, kiss passionately and whisper sweet words of endearment' experience I dreamt of. He was agitated.

My future husband stayed with me for two weeks and it was wonderful. At the end of the fortnight, we decided that he would stay on.

'I want to give up my life in the US for you,' he said. 'I'm not going back there to live.'

You could imagine how loved I felt! My loneliness quickly dissipated. He also became my protector as my husband would randomly turn up… He was my American hero.

We were engaged three months later, just after my divorce was final. He proposed on the Maid of the Mist cruise under Niagara Falls. It was very romantic. Children were discussed, along with my 50/50 chance of passing on Crouzons. He wanted children.

'You turned out great so why won't they? Let's go for it,' he said.

I had desired children since my early 20s but my first husband hadn't and he'd encouraged me to study my Master of Education instead.

We started trying for a child before the wedding. I had endometriosis so I was warned by my gynaecologist that I might never conceive … but to my shock and delight I did, instantly.

The wedding was a fairytale. We stood holding hands, gazing lovingly into each other's eyes under a shady tree beside a shimmering and glistening lake. We released snow-white doves which flew in a circle above us to the refrains of a harpist. Our honeymoon was up the coast in a friend's unit.

We'd only been in the unit a couple of days when I knew there was a problem with the baby. I was bleeding. We raced back down to my obstetrician who ordered an ultrasound. Devastatingly, I was miscarrying at eleven weeks. A blighted ovum.

We kept trying and our first child was born in 2001, a girl, Melissa (now called Maeve). Maeve had feeding issues and not being able to stop her crying sent me spiralling downwards into post-natal depression. I saw myself as a bad mother. For goodness sake, I was a highly intelligent human with a Masters degree and I couldn't stop my baby from crying!

Once the feeding issues were sorted, Maeve and I settled down and I adored her along with my role as her mum. Anger like a wounded lion enveloped me when I had to go back to work full-time when she was only three months old. She was so tiny.

We didn't want Maeve to be an only child so we tried for baby number two. Nothing was happening as my cycle was erratic so I commenced fertility treatment. To our delight, I became pregnant … but again miscarried the baby at eleven weeks gestation in early 2003. The baby's heartbeat had been beating strongly just two weeks before so this loss, along with grieving my darling dad's sudden passing from a heart attack, doubly devastated us.

I lay on the trolley outside of the operating theatre sobbing, 'I just lost my dad and now I've lost my baby. I thought this baby, my 'little Viv', was a connection to Dad.'

In 2004, our son Nicholas blessed us. Like so many things in my life, his birth was stressful. My waters broke three weeks early in the middle of the night during a thunderstorm. We didn't have a babysitter for Maeve so we woke her up to take her with us to the hospital. My husband stayed in the waiting room with her. Nicholas was delivered by emergency c-section and I waited for his cry. There was none. A chill like being packed into a freezer enveloped me and I screamed, 'What's wrong with my baby?'

There was no response.

'What's wrong with my baby? Is he alive?' I shouted.

Still no response.

Tears flowed down my cheeks. *No, not again!*

A nurse appeared by my side. She stroked my arm. 'He's okay.'

'He hasn't cried,' I sputtered. 'Are you sure? Can I see him?'

'Yes, he's fine. Here he is.'

Little Nick was brought over and placed on my chest. He had been born blue and needed his airways cleared and oxygen—but he was a fighter and okay. I cried with happiness.

Both children, Maeve and Nick, were born with Crouzon syndrome.

At two weeks old, we took Maeve to the Brisbane Mater Hospital Craniofacial Clinic. Even though I hadn't been in that clinic room for fifteen or so years, I knew where I was as soon as I entered the doors. Everything was the same including the pictures on the walls, with my childhood favourite of Mickey and Minnie Mouse and their friends in a jalopy. Even my clinic nurse and my neurosurgeon were there. They welcomed me back.

It was weird.

With the sights, sounds and smells of my childhood stirred up, all those memories I had squashed down into the 'pre-1985 never to be opened again' box resurfaced. The box, though Gaffer taped up, snapped open.

Boom! Wham! Triggers, general anxiety and panic attacks became my constant companions—and I did not seek any form of psychological help.

Just like me, Maeve required life-saving skull expansion surgery as a baby for her craniosynostosis. At seven months old, she went under the knife. I recall sitting in that theatre waiting room biting all my fingernails off and pacing back and forth. The surgery took most of the day. Other parents and carers of surgical patients would come and go while we sat waiting.

Once Maeve was settled in PICU, we were led through the doors, past cots and beds with curtains and an array of machines. Hushed voices spoke. At Maeve's bedside, my heart broke and tears flooded down my cheeks. This was my fault! I'd given my syndrome to her. My baby girl, hooked up to multiple tubes, bags of fluids and beeping machines, lay asleep. Her skull was wrapped like a turban and her eyes were beginning to look like she'd gone ten rounds in the ring. My dad, who stood with me, sensed my distress. He wrapped his arm around my shoulder and whispered, 'You looked worse than that.' This comment, in a weird way, wrapped me like a warm blanket, comforting me.

We tried to give Maeve and Nick as normal a childhood as possible but everywhere we went they were stared at, pointed at and comments made about their faces.

Sometimes I would place a baby blanket over their prams when I was triggered or feeling vulnerable so no one could see them.

At the park, children refused to play with them, others laughed at them and others called their siblings over to look at them. At school, they were sometimes called names, asked rude questions and rejected. Teachers tried to educate the children from early on—but kids can be mean.

It hurt me every time I witnessed an event, like a knife stabbed in my heart. My heart became full of holes stitched up with love. I quickly learnt that attitudes, prejudices and discrimination hadn't changed since my birth.

When Maeve was around two years old, I wanted to find someone else in the world with Crouzons. I found a group on Yahoo. Upon introducing myself and hearing the other participants' stories—mums with children who also had Crouzons—tears flowed down my cheeks and happiness coursed through me. I had finally, after more than thirty years, connected with other people like me and they completely understood how I was feeling and what I was experiencing!

I set up an Australian website called, 'Our Faces Australia', with the hopes of starting a charity in Australia for facial differences as none existed (and still doesn't)—but I didn't have the self-confidence to garner financial support for it to succeed. When Facebook launched, I set up the International Crouzon Syndrome Support Group which was the first page supporting Crouzons, an Australian support group for Crouzons and the Our Faces Australia group—but I have since closed all these pages.

When the children were four years and one year old, we decided that we needed practical and emotional support. This Crouzon syndrome journey was too hard to do on our own with only my mum's help—so we joined a friend's church.

This decision reignited my faith.

My third child was conceived, on a whim, as my 'big-four-oh' approached. I saw my womb shutting—a bit like a midlife crisis, I guess. I was pregnant within the month. My easiest conception and I would have to say meant to be as, within that month, I'd decided that it was an unwise decision to have a third child and was going to go back on birth control.

We went into the birth believing Jessica had a mild form of Crouzons or nothing. Instead, at four weeks old, she was diagnosed with three copies of chromosome 21 (Trisomy 21)—she had Down syndrome. (Based on the scans, Down syndrome had been ruled out though I wasn't told that the twelve-week blood test showed I had a 1-in-5 chance.)

If we hadn't had the craniofacial syndrome, I am sure the diagnosis would have been made at birth or soon after. The two syndromes present in a similar fashion which apparently caused some confusion—but I saw her almond-shaped eyes straightaway.

This diagnosis scared the bejeebers out of me because I didn't know anything about Down syndrome and I'd internalised from the obstetrician and society that Down syndrome was a bad thing for a person to be born with. After my daughter was diagnosed, the many, 'I'm sorrys', given by friends and other medical professionals, didn't help. I received a welcome pack from Down Syndrome Queensland and wanted to vomit. I threw the information book away without opening it and plunged headfirst back into post-natal depression. I was also livid at God for allowing all my children to be born with medical conditions. Where was my regular, typical, run-of-the-mill child?

Jessica had her own health needs. Initially, she had feeding issues and then, at six weeks of age, we learnt she had three holes in her heart (AVSD PDA – atrioventricular septal defect + patent ductus arteriosus) and would require open heart surgery as a baby.

My children in 2007

Witnessing my distress, my church sent me to see a Christian counsellor and I worked through some things with her guidance. It took me a year to come to terms with Jessica's diagnosis and that my life, along with my family's, was taking a very different direction to what I planned.

As my children grew up, my life became filled with being a mum, a wife and a teacher. My husband settled comfortably into being the carer but my heart was often torn between work and yearning to be at home. Tears often flooded my eyes and anger filled my heart when I learnt that I'd missed a 'first'—a first step, first word etc.

I spoke earlier about taking Maeve, as a two-week-old, to the craniofacial clinic. Nick followed in his sister's footsteps. Jessica had her own set of specialists. For some therapies, like ENT, ophthalmology and paediatrics, we got the 'family deal' as I called it—all three children seeing the same doctor in the one appointment.

Life became a web of frequent appointments, therapies and surgeries.

All three children underwent major surgeries—from skull and facial reconstructions to Jessica's open heart surgery at eight months. From 2001 to 2021, my children underwent twenty-six surgeries which did not include the other procedures such as scans and diagnostic procedures like MRIs, CT scans and gastroscopies which they were anaesthetised for.

I took leave from work for each procedure and surgery and I'd stay in the hospital with my children. From the moment we arrived to the moment we left, I'd be at their bedsides. My husband refused to stay overnight, even when I was exhausted and wanted a brief break. Mum rarely came to the hospital due to her own triggers and, before joining a church, few people visited. It was a lonely time.

As you could imagine, life was hard, stressful and emotional. It was made harder by non-understanding parents at school who would complain to the principal about my absences. He would then give me a tongue-lashing. There was no empathy.

My mental health, which was always rollercoastering, plummeted like a lead balloon when Jessica was two years old and, on the advice of my GP, I began taking anti-depressants.

In 2013, my poor mental health, lack of self-care and trying to be everything to everyone came to a head.

In January 2013, Nick finished a four-month process of having the facial bones in the middle of his face brought forward. It's called a Lefort III surgery (Maeve had previously had the same surgery). It is highly stressful for parents and a painful process for the patient. I won't go into the details but, if you would like to know more, see my YouTube videos:

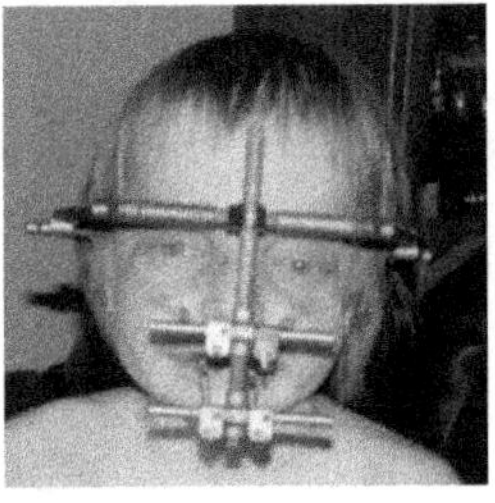

Nick's Lefort III by RED (Rigid External Distraction) – midface advancement

Melissa's (Maeve) Lefort III Mid-face Advancement using the RED Halo (youtube.com)

Nick's Lefort III Mid-face Advancement with the RED Halo 2012-2013 (youtube.com)

My anxiety became so severe there were days when I could not get myself out of the house to go to school. My stomach was a mess, my sleep disrupted, I was covered in hives and Staphylococcus skin infections and my nerves were frayed. My final day of teaching saw me curled up in a foetal position in the corner of my classroom while students belligerently ran amuck.

I immediately took leave. My GP, who had watched the decline of my mental and physical health, refused to sign my return-to-work papers if I had to go back to my classroom.

When I spoke to the principal about possible options, she said, 'You'll have to return to your class.' I then had an interview with the Education Department's psychiatrist who labelled me as having Generalised Anxiety Disorder and Clinical Depression. He also agreed I mustn't go back to the classroom. Without principal support, and no other position available for me in the school, I was forced to resign and my 25-year teaching career was suddenly over. I was granted a total and permanent disability (TPD) payout and went on a government disability pension.

Part of my recovery required seeing a psychologist. With insightful questioning, it wasn't long before the many traumatic experiences of my life were laid bare. Each one was like a weeping sore that needed to be cauterised.

I didn't cope well with leaving teaching. In my mind, when I went on leave, I'd have until the end of the year off work and start afresh the following year. My grief and even embarrassment of having to stop teaching so abruptly was exacerbated each time I walked through the front school gate to pick up my children or to attend school events. Parents would often stop me and ask, 'When are you coming back? Are you coming back next year? I want you to teach my son/daughter.' It was hard.

Searching for a new identity, I took on a few part-time jobs and decided to study youth work. My desire to be a school chaplain did not come to fruition (I believe due to my low vision and TPD payout) so I next studied a Certificate IV in Training and Assessment. It also led to a dead end.

Still on the search for self, I decided to undertake some online courses on writing and art therapy. This led me to the reignition of my childhood passion of creative writing and I joined several writing groups. My first middle grade/YA novel, Ride High Pineapple, was published in 2016 and endorsed by the Children's Craniofacial Association (USA). The main character, Issy, has Crouzon syndrome. This story was hard for me to write as I based Issy on a mashup of Maeve and myself. I continued writing novels about being different, which blossomed into school author visits. I then expanded my knowledge to writing short stories. I established local author events in my area and started volunteering at church and on my children's high school P&C. Later on, I studied life coaching and professional speaking and expanded my volunteering to Special Olympics, Guide Dogs and the Queensland Writers Centre. To date, I have written eight middle grade/YA novels and been published in 22 short story anthologies.

After leaving teaching, life at home also changed. I soon took over most of the household duties, medical appointments and taking the children out for fun activities—as my husband told me he didn't want to do them anymore. I didn't realise at the time that he was self-medicating his own demons and burgeoning depression with pornography, red wine and chain smoking.

By 2018, my husband had fully checked out on the family, the addictions having taken a stranglehold on him. My encouragement for him to seek help fell on deaf ears.

This situation meant I was going to most places on my own. With my low vision and lack of peripheral vision, I immediately encountered problems. I face-planted into the train, would walk into people, fall down stairs, trip over, receive shocks when people would come from my sides, stress out when my children would suddenly disappear and I didn't know where they were etc. To put it mildly, going out without my husband was stressful.

Towards the end of 2018, I decided that I needed to get help. I'd been supporting Guide Dogs with donations through the years and thought that I was possibly eligible for a white cane, also called a long cane. Nobody had ever mentioned the use of long canes so I was unsure. With nerves racing up and down my spine, I rang Guide Dogs and explained my situation. After submitting the medical form, I immediately commenced training with an orientation and mobility instructor.

I found learning to use the cane easy but my initial excitement wore off. Once I actually held the cane in my hand and walked up and down the footpath outside my house, swinging it back and forth, I felt as if I was walking around in my underwear. What must the neighbours be thinking?!

Next, we ventured to the local shopping centre. There, curious eyes immediately started turning towards me and kids pointed, asking their parents, 'What's that?' 'What's that for?' I felt more exposed — like naked.

These kids' reactions, unbeknown to them, triggered memories of my childhood bullying. I once more became the grotesquely deformed Crouzon kid. A tsunami of trauma surged over me and I could not breathe.

It would have been so easy to put the cane away and go on pretending to be a regular person who doesn't have low vision. I'd developed my own strategies to hide my vision impairment as best as I could, although they were limiting and proving to be dangerous.

I chose to take the harder road and kept using the long cane. In fact, I decided that if I needed to use the cane then I would have coloured canes, not just a

2019 with my new pink long cane, Seymour

white one. My first cane was pink. I named it Seymour. My psychologist worked with me to reframe the triggers.

In 2019, I decided that I would fly to Sydney to attend a public speaking bootcamp at the Speakers Institute. I wanted to become a confident speaker. I found that I could speak to children but adults were difficult as my anxiety would raise its ugly head. This was the second time in my life I had travelled on my own—my first with a long cane. My need for the cane was firmly cemented on that trip.

At the beginning of 2020, with my new NDIS (National Disability Insurance Scheme) funds, I started clay lessons at Guide Dogs. Learning pottery had always been on my bucket list and I was so excited for this opportunity. My passion quickly grew, becoming an outlet for self-care and socialising with others who live with low vision or blindness.

Life on the home front was becoming a lot more difficult with my husband's addictions. His daily drunkenness was traumatising the household and he was draining the finances with his pack-a-day cigarettes and casks of red wine. I was sourcing food baskets from churches and thought we were going to lose the house. He isolated himself from the world, watched TV for most of the day and night and appeared depressed. I wanted to help him but he wouldn't tell me what was going on in his mind. Through tears, I begged and begged him to get help. He refused. Finally, I told him, 'You must get help or move out. We can't take this anymore.' He refused to do either and, instead, tried to commit suicide twice in the garage while we were home. My son found him the first time and took the noose from around his neck. I found him the second time and called an ambulance, hoping the hospital would admit him to the psychiatric ward. He told the mental health professionals in the ER, 'Everything's okay.

I won't do it again.' They believed him and sent him home. These attempts both shocked and angered me. One reason being, these events traumatised us—but he acted like nothing had happened. The tension in the household continued to rise with my eldest two being targeted more. After stepping in between Maeve and my husband a few more times, I knew in my gut that I had to be strong and not back down. I had to protect my children. I said to him, 'You must go to rehab or leave and I'm not backing down this time.' I must have looked like I was standing strong as he said, 'You find me one and I'll go.' So, I rang around and found him a spot in the local private hospital's mental health and rehab centre. Once he was in the facility, my head was clear to think things through.

On 3 July 2020, after twenty years of marriage and being told by the police and 1800Respect that I was in a domestic violence marriage, we separated and I took out a protection order. It was awful having to sit across from my husband in court. I grieved what had happened to my marriage as, with everything we'd been through, I thought we'd grow old together.

My husband chose not to fight his addictions and gave up on life. In February 2021, seven months after we separated, he died.

When I was writing my husband's eulogy, I wanted to check on some facts so I contacted his best friends in the USA to clarify them. To my shock, I found out that many of the stories he'd told me were lies. It became clear that, when we were learning about each other in the chatroom, he'd changed his past to match my 'next relationship' checklists. He must have been as desperate for love as I was. Before ever meeting me, he told me that, since childhood, he'd craved a family and a white picket fence. The more lies I uncovered, the more lay underneath.

These revelations savaged my heart even more than the addictions did as I'd proudly told people through the years, 'We never lied to each other on the Internet.' Little did I know! These revelations also helped explain many things that never quite made sense. It's been a tough road trying to come to terms with this deceit.

With the death of my husband, I became a widow and a sole mother—another identity change I've had to work through. It hasn't been easy living with low vision, raising my youngest and supporting my other children's mental health, goals and a few more facial surgeries. I am thankful to the NDIS which has been a godsend. The scheme has helped my youngest with her hobbies, sports and therapies and I've received support for myself.

With my eldest two children now having unofficially left home (they still come and go), constant organisation and problem-solving has been the key to maintaining order and minimising stress. Along with this, I've learnt to regularly do self-care activities which bring me peace and happiness.

My first art exhibition

So, who am I now?

As I sit here with my laptop, I'm a widowed, sole parent and carer who is in a healthy new relationship. I live with low vision and anxiety and depression. I love my writing, pottery and volunteering. I am strong, brave and resilient and wary of being mistreated and lied to. I often push myself out of my comfort zone but, at times, the scared, shy, insecure little girl with the low self-esteem appears. As a Christian, I hold on to my faith. In the Bible, it says that God has good plans for those who love Him and are called according to His purpose and that He will never leave us or forsake us. Of course, I have questioned God, been angry at Him and frustrated but, as my life has evolved, I have seen my Heavenly Father helping me along the way and blessing me even when I thought He wasn't there.

Life is all about choices and I've chosen to look back at my life and see it as a tapestry. The multi-coloured, intertwined threads are the good and bad experiences. The golden threads are my life lessons. Now, I could choose to see some of these golden threads as regrets … but I believe everything happens in life for a reason, so I have chosen not to. If I didn't have those golden threads, I wouldn't have the wisdom I do today and I wouldn't be writing this book.

In conclusion, you could call me an expert and an advocate for people living with disability and differences because, as you have seen from this brief overview of my life, that is what I know. I've no clue what it's like to be regular, average, non-medical or even popular. With this life experience, as well as my studies and experience in education, youth work and life coaching, I'm well equipped to share with you what has helped me to embrace who I am and lead my best life.

Within these pages, you'll find practical strategies and ways of thinking, combined with my personal stories which have helped me to be the best version of myself … the weirdly wonderful me.

I'm frequently told that I'm an inspiration … so let me inspire you.

Before you continue through these pages, I must state that I'm not a doctor or a psychologist so please seek medical advice if you are feeling depressed or overwhelmed with life. There's professional help available. Don't be embarrassed to reach out.

Let me leave this introduction with the famous quote by Steve Jobs, Apple Co-founder:

Here's to the crazy ones, the misfits, the rebels, the troublemakers, the round pegs in the square holes ... the ones who see things differently—they're not fond of rules... You can quote them, disagree with them, glorify or vilify them, but the only thing you can't do is ignore them because they change things ... they push the human race forward, and while some may see them as the crazy ones, we see genius, because the ones who are crazy enough to think that they can change the world, are the ones who do.

Welcome to *Be Weirdly Wonderful! Embrace your differences.*

As you read the chapters, I pray that your light will shine in the darkness, you'll rise and be the strong, self-assured, happy person you're meant to be and you'll go forward with a positive and grateful outlook, leading your best life.

Chapter 2 - Be *Weirdly Wonderfully Yourself*

'To be yourself in a world that is constantly trying to make you something else is the greatest accomplishment.'—Ralph Waldo Emerson

'Do not let your adorning be external—the braiding of hair and the putting on of gold jewellery, or the clothing you wear—but let your adorning be the hidden person of the heart with the imperishable beauty of a gentle and quiet spirit, which in God's sight is very precious.'—1 Peter 2:3-4

∞∞∞∞

Have you ever been nervous about going to an event and a well-meaning friend says to you, 'It'll be all right, just be yourself?'

Sounds simple but what if, when you are being yourself, people don't like you?

During my teaching career, many times I witnessed children who were being themselves and, because they were considered different or quirky in some way, ended up being teased, isolated, rejected and often had a few or no friends. This can also happen to adults.

Being yourself can be a difficult thing in this world.

From personal experience, I think it gets easier to become your true and best self after you leave school. Any fears or masks you put on as a child or teenager can be thrown away if you have the confidence to do so. But even if you do this, unless you have dealt with the past, you can still have insecurities, subconscious thoughts and possibly even trauma from your childhood that prevents your mind from being fully free.

For example, let's return to, 'It'll be all right, just be yourself.' You may want to be yourself but your thoughts say, 'If I'm myself, no one will like me and I'll be rejected, bullied, or lonely' or, if it's related to the workplace, 'I won't get that promotion I want.' Your worries about the consequences of revealing your true self don't permit you to unmask.

A personal example is … I hid the severity of my low vision and faked being able to see better than I actually could for the whole of my childhood, through my teaching career up until 2018 (when I turned 51!). As a child, I refused to wear my glasses as that would have added 'four eyes' to my 'googly eyes' and 'froggy eyes'. Then, as a teacher, I worried my lack of vision would be used against me. The principal and my colleagues knew I couldn't drive and I had a visual impairment—but they didn't know the extent to which I pretended I could see and that I had developed my own strategies to keep myself safe.

A meme popped up on my Facebook newsfeed recently. It said, *If I asked your dad, your best friend, your neighbour, your colleague and the checkout girl at the supermarket you shop at, they would all have their own impressions of who you are.* This got me thinking.

Even if you are being yourself, depending on where you are and who you're interacting with, people will have their own perception of you.

I know that with my youngest daughter I'm fun and silly. At Bible study, I tend to be quiet and studious. To my cousins who saw me growing up, I'm known as the loud one. To people in the street, I'm the blind one with curly hair.

If we think about our various roles and ways we behave, I believe we are the total of all of these—I am all of those observations above. And this summation is most likely fine, unless we're being a horrible person who hurts others.

In my opinion, you can try to change yourself into a totally different person but, at some stage, you will start slipping back into your true self. The mask strings will snap.

As I have already referred to in my introduction, my late husband, in his desperation to find love and have a family and a white picket fence, changed himself into who I told him over the Internet I wanted. He wrote down all my answers to his questions so he could refer to them. No wonder he was my perfect match! Once we married, more lies were spun to cover up his initial ones. The cracks eventually started to appear as he found it more and more difficult to keep up the façade. If he'd told me the truth a few years into our marriage, or even ten years in, I'd have been angry but could have forgiven him. Maybe things would have ended up differently and he'd still be alive today.

I love this quote by Mahatma Gandhi:

'Your beliefs become your thoughts,
Your thoughts become your words,
Your words become your actions,
Your actions become your habits,
Your habits become your values,
Your values become your destiny.'

When I first read this, it impacted me instantly. It clearly demonstrates that our thoughts are at the centre of who we are and what we do. Our mind affects how we deal with whatever happens to us, the values we hold dear and, ultimately, the decisions we make about our lives. There is also a Bible verse about our minds which really resonates with me. In Romans 12:2, it says, 'Be transformed by the renewing of your mind.'

What do you think that means? If something is *transformed* it is changed in a marked way. Either in its form, appearance or nature. Therefore, to transform our mind is to swap our old thinking with new thoughts. Positive ones.

For example, if my mind is full of negativity about my body, 'I have a big bum which I hate,' then it needs to be transformed. I need to change my thoughts to something more positive. 'It's big and that's okay. More padding to sit on.'

Being yourself is about accepting your flaws and your points of difference. It's about not caring what others, who don't really know you, think of you. It's about your inner qualities—being a noble citizen and helping others. And for Christians, it's about being more Christ-like.

Take your mask off—unmask.

To be leading our best life, we must be authentic and true to our uniqueness and quirks. It's these traits that make us one-of-a-kind, imperfectly perfect human beings. Instead of hiding our differences to fit in, or trying to be like everyone else, or masking ourselves to be how someone else wants us to be, we should be shining and standing tall like flashing lighthouses in the darkness.

Now, I don't want to be the Easter Bunny here. The reality is that to be ourselves is often easier said than done. I acknowledge there are many barriers standing in the way. But if you can, by the end of this chapter be more accepting of yourself and comfortable in your own skin, then life is going to be better. Here are eight things you can do on your journey to becoming your authentic self.

∞∞∞∞

'Today you are you! That is truer than true. There is no one alive who is you-er than you.'—Dr Seuss

∞∞∞∞

Kill the negative labels

From the moment we're born and as we grow up, society pins labels on us. The first one is usually boy or girl. After this, dependent on how we look, our personality and how we act, others are tacked on. For example, pretty, cute, naughty, active, quiet, tomboy, girlie, fat, loud etc.

Something I've had to do is unpack the labels society gave me. I've had to identify what negative labels were attached to me growing up and then purposefully destroy them. For example, society told me I was different, deformed and unimportant. I was called ugly, googly eyes, froggy eyes, Elephant Man and Frankenstein. That Australian Women's Weekly magazine article I told you about earlier reinforced to me as an impressionable nine-year-old that I was sub-human. No wonder I had a low self-esteem and low self-worth by the time my teen years hit!

The main reason I developed post-natal depression after my youngest was born was her label—'Down syndrome'. That Down syndrome label came instantly with a whole heap of others like a magnet attracting sharp needles. These additional labels were words like 'retarded', 'not going to amount to much', 'always happy', 'lifetime of dependency', 'should have been aborted', 'medical issues' and so on.

Reliving memories and identifying these labels can be a very painful process and I encourage you to seek the support of a professional if you need help with this. (I talk about psychologists and psychiatrists in Chapter 5 *Be Weirdly Wonderfully Balanced*.)

After these negative labels have been identified, the next step is to destroy them. Why? Because these labels were attached to pull you down and to be detrimental. You don't have to keep believing them. They *can* be replaced with positive labels and beliefs about yourself.

This killing of negative labels process is all about acknowledging what was but isn't anymore. It's about taking back control from the perpetrators so the labels will no longer hold you hostage.

Here is a practical activity for you to try. Let's destroy those negative labels once and for all:

- Write a list of your negative labels on a piece of paper or write a letter to your younger self stating the labels. (When writing the letter, tell your younger self that those labels which were said to hurt you were lies and you're not going to accept them anymore.) If you want to, you could also write a letter to a specific person who gave you the negative labels.

- Next is to actually burn the list or letters you write. Yes, put a match or a lighter to them or place them in a bonfire and watch the flames vaporise those labels. They're gone. (I have done this a few times now and I have found it to be very cleansing.) If burning isn't your thing then you could tear them up into tiny bits and send them off in the wind or float them down a creek or out in the ocean. If you're a Christian, you could nail them onto a wooden cross or pin/glue them on a picture of the cross. The healing is in the process of letting the labels physically go.

- We now want to replace the negative labels with positive words. To do this, take out a fresh piece of paper and list all the great things about yourself. For example, strong, funny, quirky, pretty. For Christians, the Bible is full of positive labels of who God sees you as. These are some examples: I am strong and courageous, I am precious, I am God's child, I am loved.

- Then write down the things you're good at, how the people who love you see you and what you like about yourself. If you're having trouble, ask trusted loved ones and friends for how they see you. And remember, the fact that you're alive means that you're meant to be here. You are meant to impact the world in a positive way, whether big or small.

- Last, display them in some way. You could write the positive labels on post-it notes and stick them on your mirror or around the house where you'll constantly see them. If you like art and craft, you could draw, scrapbook, collage, decorate the page or make your new labels into a painting. You could even make a bookmark, a fridge magnet or a picture to go in a frame. This step is crucial for two reasons. One, it celebrates how wonderful you are and two, you'll see the positive labels day after day. When you see them regularly, over time they will take root in your mind and you're more likely to believe them.

Keep your thoughts positive and focus on them

Once you've destroyed your negative labels and replaced them with positive ones, how do you think you could keep the negative labels and associated thoughts at bay?

I'm a realist and I know those negative labels will come back to haunt and taunt you. Research says we have at least 50,000 thoughts pass through our minds every day—and I know from lots of experience that, when we're having a bad day, the negative labels come and tell us how terrible we are!

Research has found there are two kinds of thought patterns and self-talk, which I will demonstrate in the following scenarios:

a) In the morning, you're tired and you catch all the red lights when driving to work. You start to get annoyed, snapping, 'Damn red lights. Grrrrr. Hurry up and turn green!' Then you yell, 'Go!' and beep your horn at the cars in front of you who don't take off instantly. You enter work in a grumpy mood and when you spill coffee on your crisp white shirt you swear and sarcastically say, 'This day just keeps getting better!' At lunchtime, you look in the fridge and your lunch has disappeared. This tips you over the edge and you stomp around the office to find the culprit. When you do find them, you give your colleague a piece of your mind. Then, at 4 o'clock, your boss tells you that you must stay back for an extra two hours but you wanted to leave on-time to go out for dinner with friends. You stay back but are in a ropable mood. (Any of this sound familiar?!)

b) In the morning, you're tired and you catch all the red lights when driving to work. Before leaving home, you put on a podcast. At each red light, you sit patiently and listen to the commentary. You're smiling and thinking, 'This is a good day and I'm in a good place'. You're happy when you arrive at the office. You still spill the coffee on your crisp white shirt but you just get a paper towel and wipe your shirt and then get back on with your job. When your lunch is stolen, you have a look around to see who has it and they apologise to you. They tell you they'll make it up to you and you run out to get some food. You're slightly annoyed but let it go. You buy yourself your favourite takeaway and a cheap top to wear. Finally, when the boss tells you you're staying back for an extra two hours, you tell him you've got plans for dinner with old friends and he decides that you only need to stay back one hour. You are a little late for your night out but something is better than nothing. Your friends all work and they understand and commiserate with you.

So, research calls these two types of thought patterns and self-talk *self-defeating* and *constructive*.

a) The first scenario above showed *self-defeating* thoughts. These are thoughts that launch us into negativity. The thoughts may include: this day sucks, I'm no good at anything, everything always goes wrong for me, things will never change, my boss hates me so he's making me stay back and I always make things worse.

b) The second scenario illustrated *constructive* thoughts. These are thoughts that launch us into positivity. They are helpful and rational. For example, I've got this, I can do this, I'll just try again, my life is going to get better, hitting all the red lights is okay, staying back I'll make some extra money and I'll still make dinner even if I'm a bit late.

To be leading our best life, we need to aim for as much positive self-talk as we can. The more days we cultivate positive and constructive thinking, the better equipped we'll be to handle those difficult, self-defeating days.

If you feel this is an area of your life that you need help with, read on. Here are some strategies to try:

Reflection. For this activity, you sit comfortably in your favourite chair. Close your eyes and take deep, slow breaths from your diaphragm (put your hands on your tummy if you need to so you can feel your lower chest going up and down). Once you're relaxed, remember the thoughts you've had that day or recently. Look at them from an observer's point of view, like a person in the street who's listening to you, not adding any emotion to them.

Ask yourself:

- Are they negative or positive?
- Are they self-defeating and tearing you down?
- Are they making you angry and in a low mood? or
- Are they positive, constructive and encouraging?

If they're negative and self-defeating, can you change them into constructive ones? If you are able, tell the negative thoughts that they're wrong and they're lying to you. Then replace those negative thoughts with positive ones. If your mind is slipping into lots of self-defeating thoughts, go and get those positive labels on the post-it notes from the last activity and read them. If you didn't do that exercise or want to do more, now would be a perfect time to do it.

And once last tip… If you have a wise friend or a support worker who can give you the positive perspective on a situation that you see in a negative way, talk to them.

Affirmations. Your affirmations are positive sentences or statements which aim to bring the best out in you. An example of an affirmation is, *No matter what seat life gives me, I can always choose to have a front row experience.* Another is, *I believe in my potential, not my past, and I am good enough.*

Here is a list of affirmations:

- My body is healthy and my mind is at peace.
- I am unstoppable today.
- No matter what comes my way, I can conquer it.
- I've been given endless talents which I can use every day.
- My mind is full of joy and happiness.

- I am strong, brave and courageous.
- I can stand up for myself.
- I am valuable and have a job to do on Earth.
- Kindness is my friend.
- I radiate beauty and grace.
- I choose to forgive others who have wronged me.
- I am worthy of my dreams.
- I believe in myself.
- Every day my mind is filled with new ideas.
- I don't fail, I learn a lesson.
- My mind is full of gratitude for being alive.
- I love and accept myself unconditionally.
- I have the power to achieve my goals.
- My mind is focused.
- I am worthy of all the good things life has to offer.
- I will accept all the wonderful things coming my way.
- I am a child of the most-high God.

Put an asterisk beside five of them you like or write five of your own. Again, you could write these down and pin them up somewhere. Here is a longer example using multiple sentences:

Today will be my day.
I am the best me there is.
I know that I'm a winner.
I can do it. I know I can.
God will always be with me.

Visualisation. Visualisation is where you close your eyes and use your visual memory to see the affirmations.

If you would like to try this, make yourself comfortable and close your eyes…

- Take some deep, slow breaths from your diaphragm.
- Now, see yourself with your affirmation. For example, if it's 'I am confident' then picture yourself being confident in your stance and tone of voice.
- Then try to feel your affirmation. For example, assume the posture of confidence—sit up straight with your shoulders back and your chin up.
- Finally, speak your affirmation out loud with certainty—'I am confident'.

There's also another visualisation technique that I like to do. It's great when I'm trying to concentrate on something and self-defeating thoughts keep entering my head:

Step 1: If it's safe to do so (so not while you're driving!), close your eyes and imagine a big, red stop sign.

Step 2: Say in your head or out loud, 'Stop, thought.'

Step 3: Park the thought beside the stop sign and say, 'I'll deal with this later'. If you need to deal with the thought immediately, you can change the thought into a positive one and say, 'No, I am not... I am...'

For example,

- Negative thought, 'I'm going to fail this exam.'
- Reframe to a positive. 'Stop! I have studied hard and I'll give it my best go. If I do fail, I'll go and see the teacher about how I can make up the marks.'

Morning Routines. A devotion, some worship music and prayer are a brilliant way for Christians to start a day. During this time, you can thank God for the new day and give Him your day. You can also hand over your worries and ask for what you need, like patience, strength, courage, wisdom and peace.

I have a poster in my kitchen which reads:
Hello, this is God. I will be handling all of your problems and concerns today. That's my job. Your job is to give them to me, and then to trust me. Have a great day! (Based on Philippians 4:6.)

Some people start their day with yoga where they stretch, calm their minds and are grateful. Some people go for a walk or a run. Some people have a warm shower. Some people listen to music.

Routines are personal and different for everyone so the aim is to do something or a number of things that help you start your day with a positive mindset. Waking up late and rushing out the door is what you're trying to avoid!

Don't compare yourself to others

You are unique. You're one-of-a-kind. There's nobody else in the world exactly like you. Even identical twins don't have matching fingerprints—they are different and unique.

Society likes us to compare ourselves to others. Many people go into debt, to purchase the biggest and latest and best gadgets and technology. For example, the news regularly reports massive lines of people, many camping out, so they can be one of the first to get the latest iPhone. I'd never do that so why do so many? I believe that it's often for status, to be the envy of others, to keep up with the Joneses, to be hipper or even to look wealthy.

The beauty and diet industries are huge because people compare themselves to celebrities, fuelled by the media and Hollywood. The US beauty industry is worth $445 billion in sales and the US diet industry is worth $60 billion! They want everyone to compare themselves and be unhappy.

The problem here is you'll never feel good enough if you are rating your worth by comparing yourself to others and basing your worth on things such as owning the latest technology, the name-brand clothing or the flashiest car, being ultra-muscular or having the best pose or pout on Instagram. Why? Because no matter how hard you try, there will always be someone who can do something better or has a better paid job or has more money and a seemingly better life. If you continue to compare yourself to these people or strive to be like people who aren't like you, you'll never be truly happy and be your authentic self. You won't be leading your best life.

My family and I never had the money to buy expensive branded items. I grew up with mainly hand-sewn clothes, which I loved—and my Barbie and large dolls had matching dresses! In my cupboard hung a few expensive outfits only worn at church and when I visited my doctors in the city. When I was a teen, my mother stopped making my clothes and would take me shopping. I remember being excited when Mum bought me a Choose Life t-shirt shown in Wham's music video. The only branded item I actually remember having was a light blue Puma bag in high school. My fashion sense at university consisted of men's shirts (mainly my father's) and vintage clothes from the charity shop.

I didn't have much money to spare when my children were growing up and we received many hand-me-downs from friends. Because of this history, I still don't want to pay what most name-brands cost when new.

Did you know that research shows we start comparing ourselves to others at just four years old? I saw this with Maeve, my eldest, due to her facial difference. There were no issues in toddler playgroup but, upon entering kindergarten at the age of four, the teacher told us that some of the children were reacting negatively to her face. The teacher immediately stepped in and implemented a learning unit on faces and how they're the same and different. That strategy helped immensely and Maeve didn't have any more issues until primary school.

In Year Two, at the primary school where I was teaching, she started being asked by the other Year Two children, 'What's wrong with your eyes?' and being told, 'You have big eyes.' As naïve parents, we hadn't prepared her for this. Thinking it was the best parenting strategy, we'd treated her like she was an ordinary child and not made a fuss about her prominent, wide-spaced eyes. Maeve didn't know how to respond to the sudden barrage of taunts and questions and her mental health and behaviour took a turn for the worse. We ended up taking her to a psychologist to help her understand her difference and to encourage her to have positive labels.

A while ago, I saw a TV advertisement showing a woman entering a lift filled with mirrors and then taking multiple selfies from different angles. I remember the ad because it struck me how much it reflected many people who spend a great deal of time posing to capture their best and most attractive self. They take multiple photos and then use filters and photo editing apps to make themselves look 'perfect'. Maybe you can identify with this.

I'm not surprised that research conducted on the effects of social media on appearance clearly showed social media can be toxic. As most of us are aware, appearance is often shown as central to success on social media and collecting 'likes' and followers is seen as a mark of achievement and popularity. And the number of likes and followers collected can directly influence feelings of self-worth. Many users on these platforms ache for compliments and, when negative feedback or criticism occurs, they either can't cope or they try even harder to outdo others.

This obsession with finding worth on the Internet will always hinder a person from being their authentic self.

I used to be guilty of feeling jealous of others on Facebook—but that wasn't for their looks. Having a tight budget and living on a low salary, I'd see the holidays and all the great things people were doing and my green monster would come out to play along with my self-defeating thoughts. In the end, I had to either leave Facebook or change my attitude and see the platform for what it was. I decided to change my attitude, regularly reminding myself that many people only post the best parts of their lives. Most people weren't airing any of their problems or mistakes or insecurities.

Research by media scholar Dr. Jennifer Lewallen confirms the conclusions I have made from my own observations. She identified that the constant bombardment of images and updates of others succeeding financially, socially, educationally etc. on social media can make a woman feel she just isn't good enough and that she constantly needs to change something about herself to be better. Lewallen also found that this impact happens for the reasons I proposed— that people tend to use social media as a highlight reel rather than a reflection of their whole or real life.

It's wise to protect your thoughts and self-worth when using social media. Don't let the constant negativity and shallowness of what you see on the platforms stop you from being your true self.

Find your inner child

What do you think 'find your inner child' means? Is it doing the things you did as a child such as playing at the park? Is it being defiant and deliberately breaking rules? Is it pigging-out on lollies?

When I say, 'find your inner child', I'm not talking about breaking the law or taking on childish or irresponsible behaviour. Instead, I'm suggesting that you try to not get hung up on all your adult responsibilities. I'll help you unpack this.

As bills stack up, work stresses you, the day-to-day grind of kids' homework and after-school activities tire you and general fatigue from life takes hold, it's easy to slip into becoming almost zombie-like with a low mood. I know this is happening to me when I stop smiling, laughing and singing.

I have found that one of the best ways for me to pull myself out of the bog is to go back to pursuing simple pleasures—and the majority of these are things that brought me joy as a child.

If I wrote a list of the activities that I remember loving as a child, I'd find that reading, writing stories, doing craft, imaginative play, hanging out at the local creek, swimming, the beach, camping, riding my bike, playing boardgames and listening to music would be included.

I don't ride a bike anymore due to my eyesight but I do walk along the creek near home, go to the beach, listen to music, read, write stories and play Scrabble. These things which I did as a child still bring me joy and pleasure. These activities help to fill my energy levels, build my well-being and bring happiness.

Can you think of two or three things you could do? Maybe doing cartwheels or climbing trees will now be out of the question! And can you incorporate them into your daily, or at least your weekly, routine? Maybe you loved swimming as a child—can you get back in the pool? Maybe you loved Lego—is that something you'd like to do again? I know these things can make a difference to your mood.

I learnt about keeping your inner child from my dad. I loved his fun, silly side. He sang, he body surfed and he joked about—but he was also a totally mature, serious man. I have a goofy photo of him at my wedding wearing a tiny top hat which was a decoration. Remembering it always makes me smile.

Karen Wilson (2019) says on page 226 of her memoir, *The Inside Story*, 'You may have been told that children should be seen and not heard, but it isn't true. The child within you needs to laugh out loud, to sing, to shout and to be known for the wonderful way they are made and the amazing things you are capable of. Just step out and do some of those things that bring you happiness and your true self will shine'.

Follow and develop your hobbies, passions, talents and strengths

Everyone is good at something. Everyone has some type of talent. If you say you're not good at anything, I believe you just haven't found your 'thing' yet.

I'm not saying that there's something that you'll be perfect at as soon as you try it—that rarely happens for anyone—but I believe there is a talent that you'll be able to develop which other people find difficult to do.

Many people, including myself, have tried doing something once and not been great at it or even failed and then said, 'I'm no good at that,' and not tried again. If you think about professional athletes and their talents, it's clear that excellence comes with practice. How many laps do Olympic swimmers swim each day, following that never-ending black line? How many balls do tennis players hit over the net? How many golf balls do pro-golfers whack? How many hours do you think surgeons have spent practising? Skills can be developed. I'm sure you get the idea.

Now is confession time again for me. As a school teacher, I thought I'd be able to write a children's novel in one draft and it would be super fantastic and award-winning. How wrong I was! My first story was critiqued by fellow children's authors and was torn apart and basically called rubbish. I left that meeting in tears, feeling very disheartened! I could have just thrown in the towel and stopped but I enjoyed writing so much and I'd been writing stories since childhood. My heart was deeply hurt but I realised that I wasn't as good as I thought and that I needed to improve. Since then, I've worked hard and become an Amazon best-selling author and writing is very satisfying to me.

Robert Vallerand, a researcher from the University of Quebec in Montreal, conducted a study with associates on the benefits of having a passion or hobby. The research concluded that participating in a passion can add eight hours of joy to your week. And this joy is the best kind of happiness—it gives gratification and a lasting sense of fulfillment.

Pursuing a passion or hobby gives you time to refill your emotional energy cup and, if the activity involves other people, it also provides social connections and friendships. I can attest to gaining this from my weekly activities.

If you don't have a hobby or interest and you're wanting to find one, go and try different things. You'll obviously need to ensure you're financially able and to remain true to yourself. For example, if you hate dancing then you probably shouldn't sign up for a jive class but, in saying that, be open to at least trying new activities you may have never considered.

The Merriam-Webster dictionary defines a strength as *a strong attribute or inherent asset.*

What are your strengths? For example, are you good at problem-solving or are you compassionate, logical, pragmatic or a great communicator? More examples include leadership, humour, honesty, gratitude, kindness, teamwork, social intelligence and self-control.

If you're unsure what your strengths are, there are assessments you can do. As part of my speaker training, I completed the Gallup Clifton Strengths Assessment with the results indicating that connectedness, learner, achiever, intellection and focus are my top five strengths. I've since reflected on what these mean and I agree.

My first power, connectedness, is my belief in God and that everything happens for a reason. Learner is obviously that I love to learn new things and that I have a constant desire to achieve. Next, I love intellectual activities. I'm really not into frivolous conversations but would much rather have a deep and meaningful one. Finally, I'm very focused on my goals and whatever job or activity I am doing.

Even without a formal assessment, it's still a useful exercise to think about, and write down, what your strengths are. If I hadn't done a professional assessment, I would have said my strengths were honesty, kindness, fairness, a learner, faith, determination, bravery and creativity. These attributes make up the real me.

Develop and work on your strengths.

Learn from your mistakes, they don't define you

Another confession I must make is that, for far too many years, whenever I made a mistake, when things didn't work out perfectly or I said something wrong, I would psychologically beat myself up.

For example, I would get angry when I found one mistake in one of my preview copies of my books. Another was what I termed 'foot in mouth disease' where I'd say something without thinking and upset someone. There were many more, too numerous to share. I deeply regretted some mistakes.

I'm sure you can identify with this. We've all been affected by our mood, hormones, financial pressures, circumstances etc. and made mistakes.

A specific mistake that clearly stands out to me from my teenage years occurred at my first-and-only organ recital. I'd been learning to play the organ and my teacher put on an end-of-year recital in the local church hall. I wasn't great at practising but I thought I knew my piece well. When my name was called, the butterflies began to flap and fly around, bumping into each other and crashing to the floor of my guts. I felt all eyes on me as I walked up the steps onto the stage. I shuffled onto the wooden stool at the organ, my hands trembled and my head spun. I started the piece and fumbled over some notes. My butterflies immediately spun, tumbled and fell. Wings were torn off and lay scattered. I tried again. I couldn't get the rhythm right. Heat flushed my face. I tried again. I made another mistake... I wanted to die. I eventually made it through, received a clap and, with a bright red face, slunk back to my seat. The next student, my friend, played her piano piece to perfection. I wanted the wooden floor to open up and swallow me.

Some mistakes are small and we can easily let them go. Others have more profound effects on us. Even though the above event was traumatic for me, in the scheme of life it was small. Probably no one else even remembers it.

Other mistakes have more significant consequences or can even be catastrophic and life altering. It's these mistakes, which sometimes become regrets, that can stop us from being our true selves and leading our best life.

So, let's now talk about regrets. *'Regrets, I've had a few. But then again, too few to mention.'* These lyrics are from Frank Sinatra's song 'My Way'.

How do you see regrets—are they helpful or harmful? Personally, I've never thought of regrets as being helpful but interestingly, regret research has found that they can be helpful. Why? Well, the research reports that regrets can teach us a lesson we shouldn't repeat. Can you see the helpfulness in that?

∞∞∞∞∞

'Fear of making mistakes is in itself a huge mistake, one that prevents you from living, for life is risky and anything less is already loss.'—Rebecca Solnit

'If you have the guts to keep making mistakes, your wisdom and intelligence leap forward with huge momentum.'—Holly Near

∞∞∞∞∞

With age, I've learned to reframe past mistakes, much like the regret research suggests, turning them into learning experiences. Instead of self-criticism, I can take an objective look at what happened, extract a life lesson, then apply it to my future with the aim of not repeating the mistake.

Another simple example of this occurred recently when I was cleaning out my garage in semi-darkness. I tripped over one of the kids' small bikes with trainer wheels, overbalanced and fell down, landing on the concrete floor and hitting my face. My glasses broke and cut my eyebrow as they flew off. I knew if I called out, no one from upstairs would hear me so I lay there for a while before I gingerly pulled myself up. This fall scared me and my eye became swollen and bruised.

I looked at the situation and thought, 'That was a stupid thing to do. What do I learn from this?'

I didn't beat myself up, which is what I would have done in the past. In the past, I would have labelled myself, 'You stupid woman. You're such an idiot.'

The obvious answer to my question was … don't clean out the garage at night when the light is poor or until I get new lights installed. Other lessons I learnt included: make piles, put items like bikes in a different area and have clear walkways to reduce my risk of tripping or slipping.

We all make mistakes, so be kind to yourself.

Don't stew on the 'have nots'

My life has been influenced by my low vision. If you offered me a million dollars or my eyesight fixed so that I could drive, I would choose the latter. I'm not one of those saints who say, 'I wouldn't change a thing'. I definitely would—but I can't. There is no surgery that will fix my vision.

Not being able to drive has affected my life from the age of sixteen. It dictated where I went to university, where I lived (near public transport, shops and schools), what jobs I could do (many jobs require you to drive), how much time it takes to go places and do things, what things I do or don't go to and how independent and ultimately how in-control of my life I've been. As a sole mother who cannot drive, many extra hours are used up walking or waiting for and taking public transport. I'm thankful for support from the National Disability Insurance Scheme (NDIS) but having to rely on this means continual planning and organising support workers and transport for activities. If I could drive, this would be 'just jump in the car and go'. With the inability to drive, there's no 'let's go to the beach' on a whim — it all takes planning.

While I'm appreciative of friends taking me places, even if it's somewhere they were going anyway, I'm on their timetable and not on my own. I can't just say, 'I have to leave now,' and go like sighted people do when they want to go early. I leave when my ride is ready.

This was something that happened at my late husband's funeral — my ride was ready to go but I was still chatting with my extended family. She told me she was leaving and for me and the kids to come. I didn't want to leave and the situation became really awkward. This was my event, not hers, and I ended up telling her to go and we would find our own way home.

If you have a licence, don't take it for granted … you are blessed!

Maybe, just as I have, you've felt that others have it better than you. Maybe you feel jealous that your friend's grass is greener, as the cliché goes?

I know from speaking to others that we often think, 'If only I had their money,' or, 'If only I had their marriage,' or, 'I'm just as smart (or pretty or talented) as them so why haven't I achieved what they have in life?'

We often think that people who have wealth or fame are incredibly happy but many are not. Many sacrifice time with their family, have health related problems or have become addicted to drugs or alcohol to cope with their lifestyle.

Research shows that suicide among celebrities is significantly higher than the general population. Some people would find that surprising. There are numerous reasons for this higher percentage but the general thought is that what they're doing isn't giving them deep satisfaction and happiness.

If I spent my whole life dwelling on what I'm missing out on then I'd be a terribly cranky, always depressed and miserable person. Instead, like learning from my mistakes, I've had to reframe my thinking. I've had to consciously accept, like Paul's thorn in the flesh in the Bible, that this is my lot in life. God's allowed me to have Crouzon syndrome and low vision for my life purpose. I must accept it and live my life as fully and with as much happiness as I can. When anger or jealousy creep in, I consciously push them away.

Your 'have not' may be that you're renting and you desperately want to buy a house. Your 'have not' may be that you desire a baby and you can't fall pregnant. Your 'have not' may be that you are estranged from your family. There are so many 'have not' scenarios.

These 'have nots' and other issues (which can be financial, psychological, physical or spiritual) have the ability to prevent us from doing or having what we would really like. They can stop us from being our best and authentic self.

So, what do you think we should do to stop the 'have nots' from ruining us? Research says there are three ways:

- accept the situation/'have not'

- make ways to change it so your 'have not' becomes a 'have' or

- deal with it in some way, for example, get a second job so you 'have' enough money to go on a holiday.

If you have a 'have not' in your life that you're stewing over, how about you write it down. Then you can speak to it saying, 'Enough is enough! I'm *not* going to let this … steal my happiness anymore. I'm going to… (accept, make changes or deal with it).'

Educate people

Being born with a rare craniofacial syndrome has meant a lifetime of explaining to an array of people what the syndrome is and what it means. Doctors usually think I have thyroid issues, not a craniofacial syndrome, and they ask if my tracheostomy scar is from thyroid surgery.

Even today, many nurses and doctors say they haven't heard of Crouzon syndrome. This surprises me because it's becoming more common—and you'd hope they're educated on craniofacial syndromes at university.

When my children were born, I found myself doing a lot of advocacy for them and explaining to interested and curious people what was happening to their skulls and faces. Until I'd fully worked through my insecurities, trauma and, I guess, embarrassment of having the syndrome, I'd suffer panic attacks when talking about the syndrome. I'd start to tell someone and I suddenly couldn't breathe. I'd gulp in the air to try to get the words out and my heart would start to thump like a bass drum. It was frustrating at the time because I wanted to tell people but my unresolved psychological trauma was affecting my bodily responses. It took me many years to embrace my facial difference and be able to explain the syndrome to people without any anxiety.

It can get annoying and even tiring when you're constantly having to explain your disability or difference. I have some friends with low vision and their eyes are turned inwards or outwards. I know they get fed up with people's rude comments about their eyes and they react to the comments by being aggressive. I can understand this as it isn't anybody else's business but I personally find what works is a calm explanation, comment or just ignoring if necessary. To me, being aggressive doesn't help the situation.

I always recommend using any opportunity to educate others if they're curious. Don't take it as an insult or be aggressive or rude if people ask you about your difference. My thoughts are that attitudes won't change if we don't share what we're experiencing and how our difference affects us. I believe a large reason for prejudice and discrimination against people with disability and difference is historical segregation and the use of stereotypes. There is lingering ignorance and prejudices/bias. (I talk about prejudice and discrimination in Chapter 3 *Be Weirdly Wonderfully Victorious*.)

Stereotypes... *All* autistic people have a topic they're totally obsessed about. *All* autistic people hate making eye contact. *All* autistic people can't cope with change. Are these true? No. Autism is a spectrum and, though a person needs to have a specific set of characteristics to be given the diagnosis, everyone is not the same. Why? Well, because there are also other genetic elements and environmental factors that come into play. I always say ... if you have met one person with autism, you have met one person with autism!

As many people do think in stereotypes, it is important to educate people on what makes you, you.

Historically, people have tried to breed colour and disability out of humanity. This can be seen through the history of eugenics and Hitler where efforts were made to eradicate anyone not 'perfect'. In Australia, the White Australia Policy aimed to extinguish the aboriginal bloodline through white people interbreeding with aborigines.

In our modern era, sheltered workshops and special schools segregate. One of the trends that disgusts me the most is that many countries are trying to eradicate people with Down syndrome. In Iceland, 100% of prenatally diagnosed babies with Down syndrome are aborted, in Denmark 98%, in the UK 90% and here in Australia we are nearly as bad with 80 to 90% aborted. This makes my blood boil. How dare people decide that a person with an intellectual disability and possibly other developmental or health issues has no right to life. Most of the issues related to the high rate of terminations are caused by the medical fraternity. They are eager to 'get rid of the fetus, now'. From what I've heard, many don't give full up-to-date information on how well people with Down syndrome are doing today and they don't allow parents time to think and make an informed decision or even to talk to someone whose child has Down syndrome. The abortion is often performed on the day of diagnosis or the next. A friend of mine, who knew she was having a baby with Down syndrome, was asked if she wanted to terminate her baby by the obstetrician at a public hospital here in Brisbane—at every appointment up until her 25-week mark. I recently read an article on news.com.au of a mother in a similar position. I wonder how many babies would be aborted if there was a prenatal test for autism—probably similar numbers.

Australia is currently watching daily broadcasts of the Paralympic Games in Paris. The broadcasting, on free to air channels, is a first and shows that society's becoming better at including people with physical disabilities. Unfortunately, though, I don't believe society is as inclusive of people with intellectual disability. Did you know that athletes with Down syndrome are currently included in the Paralympics under the Intellectual Disability classification but, because they are also physically impaired, they are unable to attain the qualifying times? Therefore, these athletes cannot compete. I pray they will be given their own classification.

In my role as a children's author, I have visited schools to talk about diversity, disability and differences—and I have some lovely memories of children I met at these… The little boy who put his hand up to talk to me about his difference in the middle of my talk. I was told afterwards by the teachers that he never talked in class. The girl I noticed with the facial difference who sat quietly in the front row. I knew that, after I had left, she would be more understood. The boy with autism, sitting in the next room away from his class, who kept coming in and out of the classroom looking at me while I was giving my talk to his class. I knew we connected.

These are the simplest things we can educate others on. It isn't just about bullying and it's more than just inclusion. It's how to talk to someone who may scare us a bit because they're different and we've never seen someone like that before. It's about teaching respect for all human life, that everyone is valuable, everyone is perfect the way they are and everyone is here on Earth for a reason. And it's about seeing the gifts and talents in everyone. It's awesome that we're all different!

When I show the children my long cane and ask them what it is, I'm lucky if there is even one child who knows. Why is that? It's because they don't see many people with low vision or blindness. If they do, the person would generally be with a guide dog. After I tell them and show them how my cane works, the next time they see someone like me they'll know that person doesn't see very well.

If part of educating others involves the media, my advice is to be very careful. I've had both good and bad experiences with the media. My early experiences with print media began with the Australian Women's Weekly magazine in 1977, which I've spoken about previously. In that article on the establishment of the Australian Craniofacial Unit, the writer used archaic and barbaric language which ripped my heart apart. On a more positive note, I often appeared in the local newspaper for Girl Guides/Rangers and activities at school while growing up.

In 1990, Cher announced her Australian Heart of Stone tour. She invited some patients from the Brisbane Craniofacial Clinic to meet her. Cher, the patron of the Dallas Craniofacial Center, had become interested in facial differences while acting in the movie Mask. The Women's Weekly ran a story about three of us who would be going. Before this interview, I wasn't alerted to the dangers of the media. The story did its job of bringing attention to the work of the craniofacial clinic and Cher's tour. But a chill ricocheted up and down my spine when reading the article. There wasn't a lot about me in the story—just a paragraph—but out of all the things I'd said, they decided to print that I was nervous around the Year 7s at school due to my face. I was horrified! There were so many other better things they could have written and they chose to write about my employment! As you could imagine, lots of parents read the article and my students brought it in for 'show and tell'. I wanted to burn every copy of the magazine and it was quite a few years before the magazine disappeared.

I should have learnt from this but I didn't. My next experience was with the Take 5 magazine. In 2006, I wrote a story for the Mater Hospital for their 100 Stories centenary book. My story was on the opening of the Brisbane Craniofacial Clinic and my experiences. A writer contacted me about doing a story about me for a national magazine. I agreed, thinking it would bring awareness to Crouzon syndrome. Again, like the Women's Weekly, I was angry when I read the story and I wanted to burn every copy. Why this time? The story that I had agreed to had been changed and I hated the title. We were also put in the 'most shocking story' category with a poll asking the readers to vote on whether I should have given birth to my children! I was mortified, livid and humiliated. Soon after, Take 5 contacted me. The article was their best story and they wanted to do another. What do you think my reply was?

Burnt twice, I was reluctant to do any more media. Channel Nine saw my Take 5 story and contacted me for an online story. I was extremely hesitant but they assured me the story would be sensitive and respectful. I'm happy to say it was. This led to a TV current affairs program, Extra, running a story. Our story was the second-highest rated for that year (beaten by a story about a surfing mouse!)

A writer from Take That contacted me about five years later, after I was featured in another online magazine story to do with bullying. Take That magazine was similar to Take 5. I wanted more awareness for facial differences but was nervous and reluctant, voicing my concerns. They reassured me this story would be sensitive, have a positive headline and there'd be no polls etc. To my relief, the story was tasteful. Since that time, I've been favourably featured in local newspapers and on social media.

Just be wary!

∞∞∞∞

In this chapter, I've shared eight ways to be your true, authentic self. I've discussed the importance of killing negative labels, keeping your thoughts positive, not comparing yourself to others, finding your inner child, following and developing hobbies, passions, talents and strengths, learning from mistakes so they don't define you, not stewing on your 'have nots' and on the need to educate people about your disability or difference.

The more you can be your true, authentic self and comfortable in your own skin without wearing a 'mask', the more you will be leading your best life.

In Chapter 3, I'll being sharing my thoughts on how to be weirdly wonderfully victorious.

Chapter 3 - Be *Weirdly Wonderfully Victorious*

'The first and greatest victory is to conquer yourself.'—Plato

'Now this I know: The Lord gives victory to his anointed. He answers him from His heavenly sanctuary with the victorious power of His right hand.'—Psalm 2:6

∞∞∞∞

Have you ever felt that you're a victim of your circumstances or your disability or your race or your religion or for any other reason?

Yes? Me too. But something I've discovered on my path to leading my best life is that we ultimately do have control of our life, within the bounds of societal laws. If we think about it, we're free every day to make choices about what we do and what we think. This free will came from God and goes back to Adam and Eve.

It's amazing how many decisions we make in a day. Research says about 35,000! Can you believe it?

The Latin root of 'decision' means 'to cut off' — so we could say that making a decision is cutting off all the other choices. Some days we make decisions quickly and other days we agonise over them. Some decisions are easy to make, other decisions are harder. Some decisions require little thinking and others take time and require research or seeking wisdom from others who've been in the same situation.

Decisions make our choices.

In my life, I have found one of the hardest decisions to make is in the clothes shop change room ... which sounds rather silly. Maybe you can identify with this. I go into the shop looking for a specific item, say, a blue top. There are three, four, five, six or seven tops I like. I only intend on purchasing one of them. I try them all on and, lo and behold, there are three that I like! Which one do I choose? In my indecisiveness, I've stood in a change room for well over half-an-hour deliberating, trying clothes back on, whirling and twirling and scrutinizing and trying them back on again, whirling and twirling and scrutinizing them... I get so wound up that my heart starts to hammer. I came in to buy one... Which one, though? And you know what I do? I walk out of the store after paying for all of the ones I liked! Something that should be a simple decision for me is not.

Obviously, there are many decisions that are way more important than choosing a top and we need to take a serious amount of time to ponder over these. If you're buying a house, it would be best to slowly think it through before signing the contract. (Not like me, who bought a house on a whim and then regretted it!) Leaving a job might also need some serious thought, particularly if you don't have another job to go to.

So, how can we make good decisions that enable us to lead our best life … a victorious life?

Research says that we're programmed to make decisions based on fear, low self-esteem and lack of willpower. This means we'll often form them in fight, flight or fear mode, to help ourselves feel better or on an impulse. (Like my clothes buying!) How do you think we can make good decisions?

Here are some tips that I have found helpful for me:

- Always weigh up the pros, cons, short-term and long-term consequences and all the available options.
- Consider the financial consequences. In my change room example, when my indecisiveness is in full flight, I'm not considering how much the clothes are going to cost but I should be. I'm still not considering the cost when I hear the total at the checkout as I'm just happy that I've left the change room! It's when I get home and pull the clothes out of the bags and look at the docket that it sinks in. I then must go without other items to pay for the clothes which I didn't actually need. What I should have done was take a step away to clear my head (maybe even gone and had a coffee or browsed in another shop) until my anxiety was under control and

only gone back when I'd made the decision on which top to buy.

- Sales can be deadly. It's so easy to be sucked into spending because we're saving (40% off, 60% off etc) but, unless we actually need an item, it's better to stay away from sales. If we buy nothing, we've saved a whole lot more! (I have heard of people freezing their credit card in a cup of water so they can't use it until the ice has thawed. It takes the impulse away.)

- The other deadly 'suck in' is purchasing items online. I've found from personal experience that it's too easy to go overboard with spending. Paying with a credit card, via Paypal or Afterpay etc. doesn't hurt straight away and it's exciting when all the packages arrive. Opening a parcel is like Christmas each time. But never forget, the items need to be paid for. Financial consequences must be front-of-mind when shopping instore or online.

- There will be times when sleeping on the decision will be the best strategy. Sleeping on a decision helps your brain to process it and provides you with a calmer demeanour.

- When you've decided, have a final think about what the opposite of that decision would be. When I was considering buying a second-hand kiln, my partner asked me, 'Would you be upset if you didn't get it?' and I answered, 'Yes', because I wanted to be able to fire from home. Firing my pottery at home would mean I wouldn't have to take everything to the community kiln and then wait weeks for firing. Not being able to drive, I could see a lot of benefits to using my own kiln. The opposite of not having a kiln was my current situation.

- Pray and ask for God's guidance, wisdom and signs.
- Ask others for advice or feedback if they've been in the same position. Don't just take advice from anyone, particularly people who think they're experts but are not. Also, if your decision directly affects someone else, it's wise and necessary to discuss it with them, too.
- Finally, if you make a mistake with your decision-making, don't beat yourself up about it. You did what you thought was right at the time. Instead, start problem-solving, dealing with the consequences and investigating options. Also … learn from the mistake.

∞∞∞∞

'Only you can control your future.'—Dr Seuss

∞∞∞∞

Be victorious with the direction of your life

Decisions make our current reality, and making good decisions helps with the positive direction of our life.

Something I didn't mention above is that envisioning our future can help with our decision-making. Say we're unhappy with our current job and would like to go to university to study for a new career. In this scenario, it's wise to weigh up all the pros, cons, consequences and available options. Once we've done this and we've decided which uni, which course, how we will be able to financially afford it etc. then any further decisions can be based upon our short-term and long-term goals. Let's look at this now.

How do you set a good goal?

Goal Setting. Do you believe in making New Year's resolutions? If you do, do you keep them? The University of Scranton has researched the number of people who keep their resolutions and found that only 8% do … which means that 92% of people who set resolutions fail. That's not very many succeeding! Maybe you don't believe in New Year's resolutions but have tried something like a diet or an exercise program with high expectations and then, after a day or a week or a month or maybe even after a year, it becomes too hard or life gets in the way and you give up? If your resolutions are made with the intention of victoriously leading your best life then, instead of making a resolution, a more effective way I have found is to write a SMART goal.

A goal is a statement stating what you want to achieve, when you want to achieve it and why you want to achieve it.

Common goals are often something like, 'I want to give up smoking,' or, 'I want to get healthier.' But as these are vague and broad and more like a resolution, they tend to lead to failure.

Let me first give you an example of a SMART goal and then I'll explain the process.

I'll walk for 30 minutes every day after I drop the children off at school. I'm doing this because it will improve my fitness and mental health. I'll begin tomorrow and I will assess how I have gone in a month.

SMART is an acronym that represents a framework for creating effective goals. It stands for five qualities your goals should be: Specific, Measurable, Achievable, Relevant and realistic, and Time-bound. The SMART method has proven to be one of the most popular and effective tools for creating realistic and achievable goals. And the more realistic and achievable they are, the more likely you are to be successful.

This is how to write a SMART goal:

Step One: Make your goal specific (S)

Your first step is to decide what you want to achieve and then think about it in specific terms.

For example, a general goal could be, 'I want to eat healthier.' But what does the word healthier mean? Break the general term healthier down further. Does it mean one takeaway meal per week, taking salads to work for lunch, two glasses of wine a week etc? For this example, a more specific goal could be, 'I will drink eight glasses of water a day.'

You'll notice that in this example I've included the number eight. This is something you can measure. Other examples could be, 'Go to the gym two nights a week', 'Lose ten kilograms of weight', and, 'Cut out all sugar from my coffee'.

Next, answer the five 'W' questions about your goal: Who, What, When, Where, and Why.

After deciding *what* you want to happen, go to the *who*.

Who do you need the help of? Could it be a personal trainer? A dietitian? A buddy? Support from your spouse or family?

Then decide *where* and *when* this will happen.

Think about the location in which you'll undertake the goal and when you'll fit it into your week. If it's exercise more, where will you be—at home, the gym, the park, the local neighbourhood? When are you going to exercise? Are you going to get up earlier or walk in your lunch hour? Also, think about *how often*. You may wish to exercise three times a week, on Monday, Wednesday and Saturday, as you feel that is achievable. Then work out *why* you're setting the goal. If you don't have a pretty good reason, it's unlikely you'll achieve it.

Write down the reasons for and benefits of achieving your goal. Post them on your fridge or mirror so, if you feel like giving up, they're right there for you to see.

Also, it's important that you work out the *obstacles or requirements* for achieving the goal. Obstacles may be time-related or about your health, family constraints, financial issues or personal safety. It could even be a psychological obstacle—maybe you hate eating vegetables or you don't like the way you look in gym gear. A requirement may be that you need a doctor's clearance or you may need special equipment. If you want to achieve the goal, you need to consider how these can be worked around or accommodated.

- What do you want to achieve?
  Answer the W questions about it.
- Who is involved in accomplishing your goal? Will you be doing it on your own or will you need help to achieve this?
- What are you going to need to achieve this?
- When will you begin working towards this goal? When will this goal be completed?
- Where will accomplishing your goals come from? For example, are you taking a class?
- Why do you want to achieve this? For example, do you want to be more qualified or gain more skills?

Step Two: Make Your Goal Measurable (M)

I talked about this briefly above when I said to use numbers in your goal. A description of the desired outcome can also be used. This will make it easier to track your progress and know when you have achieved your goal. For example, you wish to lose ten kilograms. To begin, you would weigh yourself (84kgs) and then weigh yourself regularly until you've reached your goal (74kgs). Or you could say as a description, 'Fit back into my wedding dress.' Both can be measured.

Here are some questions that can help you with making your goal measurable:

- How much? For example, 'How much weight do you hope to lose?'
- How many? For example, 'How many times a week do you want to go to the gym?'
- How will you know when you've accomplished the goal?

Devise a plan to track and measure your progress. Having measurable goals makes this easy. If you wish to lose ten kilograms, and you've lost three then you know you have seven kg to go. In this planning, decide how often you are going to measure your progress. Will it be by time (for example, once a week or fortnight) or the distance run, weights lifted, number of spoons of sugar, number of drinks of water, number of hours spent writing etc. Some people like to keep a journal. You can write in this journal the results you've seen, have motivational quotes and diary your feelings.

- How are you going to measure your goal?

Step Three: Make Your Goal Attainable (A)

Think about your limitations and how committed you are to achieving the goal. You need to ensure the goal can be achieved … otherwise, you may become discouraged. Think about the obstacles you've already identified. Then consider if you'll be able to achieve your goal with them. If not, choose a different goal. For example, if you want to go to the gym three times a week but you can't realistically fit that into your schedule then don't make that your goal.

- Can you realistically implement and achieve what you need to do to achieve your goal?

Step Four: Make Your Goal Relevant and Realistic (R)

Think about if your goal is relevant to your life. Will the goal fulfil your desires or needs … or is there a different goal that's more important to you? For example, maybe you are tossing up between studying a course that will further your career and a course for enjoyment. Which would you choose?

- Is your goal something that you really want to do? Will it help you improve or change a part of your life in a positive manner?

Step Five: Make Your Goal Time-Bound (T)

This means your goal should have a deadline or a completion date. Goals can be long-term or short-term. You may also have a long-term goal broken up into shorter ones. For example, if my long-term goal is to lose fifty kilograms then my short-term goal could be to lose ten kg in six months.

Setting a deadline or finishing time helps you to stay on track. It takes away, 'I'll do it sometime.'

- What is a realistic starting date for your goal?
- What is a realistic finishing date for your goal?

Here is a full example of planning a SMART goal.

S	Is it specific?	What do you want to accomplish? *I want to lose five kg by swimming at my local pool. I can fit the laps into my schedule on Wednesday evening and Saturday morning.*
M	Is it measurable?	How will you know when you have accomplished your goal? *When I have lost five kg.*
A	Is it attainable?	How can your goal be accomplished? *By going to the pool and buying a pool entry pass. I also need to purchase new swimmers and goggles.*
R	Is it relevant and realistic?	Is this goal worth working hard to accomplish?

		Yes, as I want to lose weight and five kg is doable.
T	Is it time-bound?	By when will the goal be accomplished? *I will start next Wednesday and I'll reassess my goal in a month to see how I'm going.*

Once you have done your planning, it's time to frame your goal:

By (date) ...

I will (what you wish to achieve) ...

so that (why this is of benefit to self/organisation) ...

For example:

By 21 July, I will have started my swimming at the local pool so that I can begin my target of losing five kg.

Once you've written it, it's time to action it!

After you have actioned your goal, the next step is to evaluate or reflect on how you went. Some example questions to help with this are:

- What worked well? What didn't?
- What was easy about the goal? What was hard about the goal?
- Were there obstacles that prevented you from achieving your goal? Were there obstacles that you needed to overcome?

- Was it too unrealistic?
- Did you lose motivation?
- What would you change? What would you take into your next goal?
- Consider the time frame, the financial cost, any impact on your family and anything else that you feel is worth considering.

Once the reflection is completed, the final step is to rewrite the goal, set another goal on a similar theme or change the goal entirely. For example, you may need to design a simpler goal, take a step backwards or allow more time. Always remember that whatever changes you make are fine because you're still on the way to success. You're pursuing victory in your life.

Next, we'll look at vision boards. Maybe you've never heard of vision boards or seen one. Essentially, they're a visual representation of your goals for a year and an enjoyable way to explore and think about what you really want to achieve. Read on to find out more.

Vision Boards. As I have just said, constructing a vision board is a way of setting long-term goals—usually for a year. If you like art and craft, you'll love making one. Vision boards are constructed from any sort of board (e.g., a bulletin board) where you display images and words/quotes that represent whatever you want to be, do or have in your life. If you don't have a bulletin board then a large piece of cardboard or even multiple sheets of A4 paper will work.

An example of a vision board

To begin, have your SMART goals handy and/or answer the following questions to clarify your vision for the year.

Step One: Answer the following questions:
- What do you want in life this year?
- What do you need to achieve this?
- What are your core values that go along with this?
- How do you want to feel when these things become a reality? Happy, content, free … victorious!

From these answers, decide what your board will be about. You can focus on one area of your life, for example, you want to spend more time with your family and less time working at the office. You can have several areas displayed on your board, for example, self-care, faith, family, work and holiday.

Step Two: Gather what you need to make your vision board

How you want to make your vision board will affect what art and craft supplies you need. Here are some general ideas of things you can use but it's really up to your imagination and creativity:

- something to attach images to, such as blank art paper, poster board, large sheet of paper or cork board
- something to affix the images with, such as glue, clips, or pins
- markers, pens, paint, scissors
- colourful pieces of paper, stickers and scrapbooking or journaling supplies
- magazines or books that can be cut up
- computer and printer if using quotes or pictures from the Internet

Step Three: Find your images and words

This step involves finding images and words that demonstrate your answers to the questions in Step One. You can cut them out from magazines and books or print some out from the Internet. Use Google or Pinterest if you need to. Stamps and stickers are awesome to use for this too. If you can't find exactly what you want, you can make your own by drawing or writing on coloured paper.

When you're looking for images, ensure they make you happy and inspire you to go after your vision. If they make you jealous or resentful or put you off then they're not the right ones. For example, if your vision board is about self-care, you may want to have pictures of people walking on the beach … which you know you could do. You may not want to have pictures of people having a holiday in an exotic location that you could never afford. Or you may want to have pictures of things that make you happy, which is the feeling you want to achieve.

Once you find all the images then it's time to glue them onto board or paper. You can overlap them, draw extra words or lines, put them in different quadrants of the paper—however you want to do it. Be as creative as you like!

Step Four: Put your vision board somewhere that you can see it

Once your vision board is complete, it can now be used as a visual reminder of what you're aiming to achieve. Look at it often. Mine is pinned to my cork board on my desk so I can see it whenever I sit down to write. If you have used art paper pages, you can pin them up somewhere or put them away and pull them out from time to time. Whatever helps you connect with your desires or goals…

Step Five: Plan how you are going to make it happen

So, you have your vision board constructed for the year. With this done, the next step is to make a list of the things you could start doing to achieve your vision. These can be thoughts, feelings, emotions, choices and actions/activities.

Start with one of the things on your list, write a goal to action it and continue from there.

Ultimately, making a vision board that works is about being clear on what you want and then taking steps towards that vision and dealing with any roadblocks along the way.

Be victorious over toxic relationships – Domestic Violence (DV)

When we're leading our victorious life, we are in healthy romantic relationships where we're respected, given unconditional love and have the freedom to be ourselves. But I often feel we're so desperate for love and a partner that we don't take the time to think carefully about whether we're making a good decision and if we're being treated respectfully, without control. I put more thought into choosing my pizza toppings than my marriages (well maybe not, but you get what I mean!). I've included this section as it's extremely personal to me. My first marriage being coercive control and my second becoming abusive over time.

We all want love. We all want to be loved. Love makes the world go round, yada, yada, yada. But how many of us stop and think about the pros, cons, short-term and long-term consequences and other options when a lover presents themselves to us? Probably not many people.

I would encourage everyone to think carefully before becoming serious with someone. Don't just go on instant chemistry or the excitement because it's so very easy to slip into an abusive relationship. It's almost too easy—particularly if we've grown up being bullied or abused and have low self-worth. Those of us who were treated poorly as a child and who crave love are vulnerable to abuse. And, as I have mentioned previously, I know this all too well.

I think back to my teenage years and I cannot remember any education on healthy relationships. In school, we learnt how babies were made and genetics in science and sex education at after-school information sessions. We also learnt how to take care of babies and how to sew baby clothes in Childcraft and Home Economics. But no one spoke to me about choosing a good partner and what a healthy relationship is. I guess the role models were my parents, other friends' parents and TV families.

Because I didn't know what a healthy relationship was, I assumed being treated badly was okay. Hey, it was what I was used to! A lot of boys had treated me badly so what did it matter if a man did?

And domestic violence? I had no clue what domestic violence even was, let alone that I was experiencing it. I first heard the term domestic violence in 1999 when community announcements were shown on TV. I had separated from my husband and I remember, standing in front of the small portable TV screen in my townhouse, letting the words sink in. As they did, a cold hard chill ran down my spine and shock consumed me. That public announcement gave me a name for what I'd been experiencing for thirteen years and told me it was unacceptable. I was right to escape. Fortunately, there is now a lot of information available and organisations who can help.

What is Domestic Violence? Many people think abuse and violence is purely physical. And I must admit, once I'd heard of DV, I thought it mainly was—but it's much more encompassing, as I found out after my second marriage. I also didn't realise my second marriage was DV as it was different to my first. It was the police who told me and they directed me to the legal definition. Then as I read the definition, it was like a poisoned arrow hit me between my eyeballs. OMG I was in another abusive marriage!

I think it's worthwhile to read the definition of domestic violence from the Queensland Court's website, which is where the police directed me to:

Domestic violence is when one person behaves in a way that controls or dominates another person and causes fear for their safety and well-being. It is usually a pattern of abusive and controlling behaviour taking many forms. It happens in intimate, family or informal care relationships.

Domestic violence includes a wide range of behaviours which may include:

- *physical or sexual abuse—punching, hitting, choking, or threatening to punch or hit, forcing a person to participate in sexual acts, damaging someone's property or threatening to damage property, including hurting or threatening to hurt pets*
- *emotional or psychological abuse—stalking, repeated text messaging, making insulting comments, calling someone names, blackmailing or extorting, preventing contact with family and/or friends, controlling someone's appearance, putting them down, threatening to expose their sexual orientation*
- *economic abuse—denying, withholding, controlling or misusing money or property, or threatening to do so*
- *threatening behaviour—saying things or acting in a way to make someone feel afraid, threatening to commit suicide or self-harm, stalking*
- *coercive behaviour—forcing, intimidating or manipulating a person to do things they don't want to do, such as sign a contract e.g., for a loan, or a legal document giving another person power over their affairs e.g., power of attorney.*

It also extends to children seeing violence, like their parent being hurt, being called names, things being broken or police arriving.

Statistics from the Australian Institute of Health and Welfare states that 2.2 million Australians have experienced physical or sexual violence from a current or previous partner.

Love is strong. Love is kind. Love is respect.

Cycle of Violence/Abuse. People uneducated on DV can wonder why victims stay. I want to share with you the cycle of violence/abuse that demonstrates how the perpetrator operates and keeps the victim in the relationship.

Domestic violence doesn't start off as abuse. The relationship usually begins with excitement and an intensity of emotions but, over time, it changes with more and more of the behaviours listed above occurring. Domestic violence relationships are said to follow a typical pattern which cycles.

This cycle I am sharing, and illustrated on page 88, was developed in 1979 by Dr Lenore Walker and describes the phases an abusive relationship moves through in the lead up to a violent event and its follow-up. While researching, I found a few different diagrams but they all essentially say the same thing. The three stages of the cycle of violence are:

Phase One: Tension-building Phase
- Build Up: Tension between the people in the relationship starts to increase and verbal, emotional or financial abuse occurs.
- Stand-over: This phase can be very frightening for people experiencing abuse. They feel as though the situation will explode if they do anything wrong. The behaviour of the abuser intensifies and reaches a point where a release of tension is inevitable.

Phase Two: Acute Explosion
The peak of the violence is reached in this phase. The perpetrator experiences a release of tension. This feeling can become addictive and the perpetrator may become unable to deal with anger in any other way.

Phase Three: Honeymoon Stage

- Remorse: At this point, the perpetrator starts to feel ashamed. They may become withdrawn and try to justify their actions to themselves and others. For example, they may say, 'You know it makes me angry when you say that.'
- Pursuit: During the pursuit phase, the perpetrator promises never to be violent again. They may try to explain the violence by blaming other factors such as alcohol or stress at work. The perpetrator may be very attentive to their victim, including buying gifts and helping around the house. It could seem as though the perpetrator has changed. At this point, the person experiencing the violence will feel confused and hurt but also relieved that the violence is over.
- Denial phase (Calm): Both people in the relationship may be in denial about the severity of the abuse and violence. Intimacy increases and both people feel happy and want the relationship to continue so they ignore the possibility that the violence could happen again.
- Over time, this phase passes and the cycle begins again.

To put it very simply, it goes from good to bad, to good, to bad, to good, to bad... In the good times, it's easy to forget about the bad. When it's bad, all sorts of threats, control and even violence can occur. Due to the insidious nature of this cycle, it can be very difficult for someone to leave. When a person does leave, the most dangerous time is immediately after they do. This fear often keeps people in the DV relationship.

∞∞∞∞

'You are not the darkness you endured. You are the light that refused to surrender.'—John Mark Green

∞∞∞∞

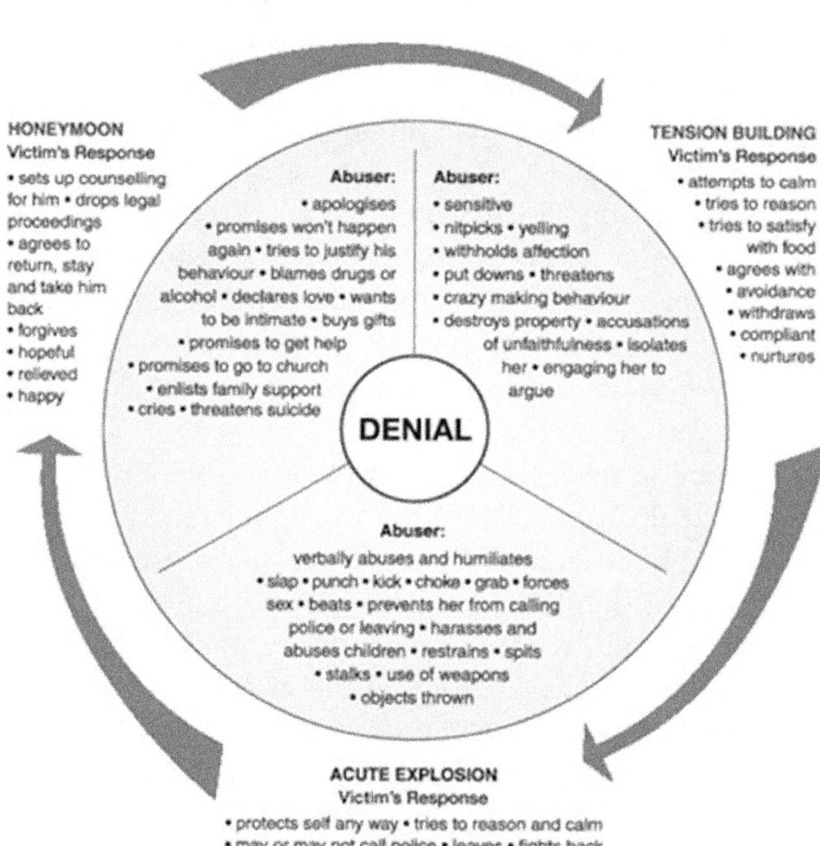

The good news is that there's help available. Please tell someone about what is going on. Australian organisations which can give advice and help you include:

- DVConnect – www.dvconnect.org
- 1800respect – www.1800respect.org.au
- White Ribbon Australia – www.whiteribbon.org.au

- Services Australia –
  www.servicesaustralia.gov.au/family-and-domestic-violence
- Domestic Violence Prevention Centre –
  www.domesticviolence.com.au
- 000 – phone the police for immediate help

What is a healthy relationship? If you want to be leading your best life, you must be in a healthy relationship. I'm now in my third relationship and it is very different to my others.

Due to my late husband's lies, I was suspicious of everything my new partner told me. He had to provide evidence to prove things such as our common interests and his divorce papers. I was fearful of heading back into another DV relationship and bringing my children along with me. My children were dealing with trauma from my late husband's abuse and I could not subject them to more. Before I could commit to being serious, I had to be sure I was making a wise and victorious decision. And to be honest, it took a while to fully commit—even though we had chemistry and much in common and he was a lovely, kind man.

So, what is different about this relationship? Why is it helping me to lead my best life?

Putting love aside, as I loved my husbands, the difference is we truly want each other to live our best lives. We want each other to feel good and to know we're both amazing people. We each want the other to be happy and to feel supported. We want to build one another up. We want to be lovers not fighters and, most importantly, friends who travel the ups and downs of life side-by-side.

Communication was always problematic in my marriages, featuring either arguments or shutdowns. Both forms are ineffective and damaging. In my current relationship, our communication is open and honest with no fear of 'saying the wrong thing'. We actively listen to each other. No topics are off the table and, when we have different opinions on something, we respect and listen to each other's perspectives.

Support for one another comes in many forms—practical, psychological and emotional. We want one another to be happy and, when one person isn't, we support them through their emotions.

We both have goals we want to achieve. Some of them are the same, others are different. We actively encourage and support one another to achieve our goals. For example, I have a goal to once a month attend a market to sell my books and pottery. I cannot do this on my own. My partner has lovingly supported me with this and comes along to help me set up and sell my wares.

We're a team. We love being together but also give one another personal space so we are free to do the things we want to do separately.

Having fun and laughing is a regular occurrence. It's been a long time since I've giggled so much.

We desire intimacy, we appreciate each other and thank each other.

My dog loves him … and, a biggie for me … we share the TV!

There are more things I could say like there are no addictions involved (this is a huge one for me), we speak kindly to each other and if we snap when we're anxious, we apologise. But I am going to leave it there.

Be a victor, not a victim.

If I've raised any concerns in your mind or you're reading this and contemplating the healthiness of your relationship then keep reading. Below are ten questions about your relationship which will give you some clues about where your relationship is at:

- Do you both have your own friends, hobbies and activities?
- Does your partner encourage you to grow?
- Do you both want the best for each other and celebrate each other's achievements and successes?
- Do you share goals for the future?
- Do you have the same financial habits/goals?
- Do you both want the same kind of relationship?
- Can you be yourself with them?
- Do you give and take from each other fairly and equally?
- Do you help, support and care for each other?
- Is your life better with them in it?

If you answered yes to the majority, you should be in a healthy relationship. If there were red flags, you may need to do some soul-searching.

A good piece of advice I wish I knew in my teens was, 'Start your relationship how you want it to end'. Why? Because generally, what is accepted in the beginning will not change. Any thoughts of, 'I'll change him/her/them after we're married', are incorrect. Your partner will only change if they want to change.

A great relationship is when someone accepts your past, supports your present and encourages your future.

Be victorious over prejudice and discrimination

When we're born with a disability or a significant difference, the world can be prejudicial and discriminatory towards us. Sometimes attitudes are subtle, other times blatantly in our face.

I have found that it's wise to know exactly what prejudice and discrimination are, how they present and what to do if you feel discriminated against.

So, what is the difference between the two? www.grammar.yourdictionary.com explains this: *Prejudice is a preconceived opinion based on prior beliefs instead of facts. It's inside someone's head. Discrimination is the act of treating someone unequally based on a perceived difference. Discrimination is a person's behaviour and how they apply the prejudice—and is illegal.*

The word prejudice means 'pre-judged'. A person who is prejudiced bases their opinions on stereotypes. They believe they already know something about a particular type of person before they meet them. They believe all people in a particular group are the same and their prejudices stop them from learning about the individual person.

In the world of disability and difference, we see this all too frequently, such as when a person:

- perceives that a person with a particular disability can't do a job
- presumes someone of colour is a thief
- is uncomfortable around gay people
- believes once they've met one autistic person they know everything about ASD

Continual acts of prejudice can affect a person's mental health by causing anxiety and depression, trauma, self-doubt in one's abilities and loss of opportunities. They go against living a victorious life. If these opinions and stereotypes are role modelled to children then the prejudices will continue to the next generation.

If one encounters prejudice, it would be beneficial to all to call it out and push back against it. Complain about the racist teacher, report the sexual harassment and the lack of access to buildings for people in wheelchairs. Society will not change while people remain silent and accept the status quo.

Discrimination occurs when a person allows their prejudice to influence their behaviour. It violates a person's civil rights. It includes rejection or exclusion.

From the scenarios above, discrimination occurs when:

- The person with the disability, who is the best qualified to do the job, is passed over for an able-bodied person (this is called ableism).
- The police are called to a crime scene and automatically accuse the person of colour.
- A gay classmate is not invited to a party.
- A person treats an autistic person like they have an intellectual disability even though they don't.

Discrimination Laws in Australia. In Australia, the following discrimination laws operate at a federal level and the Australian Human Rights Commission has statutory responsibilities under them:

- *Age Discrimination Act 2004*
- *Australian Human Rights Commission Act 1986*
- *Disability Discrimination Act 1992*
- *Racial Discrimination Act 1975*
- *Sex Discrimination Act 1984*

The following laws operate at a state and territory level, with state and territory equal opportunity and anti-discrimination agencies having statutory responsibilities under them:

- Australian Capital Territory – *Discrimination Act 1991*
- New South Wales – *Anti-Discrimination Act 1977*
- Northern Territory – *Anti-Discrimination Act 1992*
- Queensland – *Anti-Discrimination Act 1991*
- South Australia – *Equal Opportunity Act 1984*
- Tasmania – *Anti-Discrimination Act 1998*
- Victoria – *Equal Opportunity Act 2010*
- Western Australia—*Equal Opportunity Act 1984*

Commonwealth laws and the state and territory laws generally overlap and prohibit the same type of discrimination, and both must be followed.

The United Nations Declaration of Human Rights, proclaimed on 10 December 1948, was written as a common standard of achievements for all peoples and nations. It sets out fundamental human rights. The principles of equality and non-discrimination are part of the foundation of the rule of law. There are thirty articles and the human rights legal framework contains international instruments to combat specific forms of discrimination including discrimination against indigenous peoples, migrants, minorities and people with disabilities, discrimination against women, racial and religious discrimination or discrimination based on sexual orientation and gender identity.

To read the UN Declaration of Human Rights, head to: https://www.un.org/en/about-us/universal-declaration-of-human-rights - Article%202

What is Ableism? I think most people could identify or give examples of age, racial and sex discrimination. But I think disability discrimination could be more of a grey area so it's important to delve into this a bit further. I want to talk, in particular, about 'ableism' as disability discrimination goes hand-in-hand with it. From accessliving.org, the definition of ableism is *the discrimination and social prejudice against people with disabilities based on the belief that typical abilities are superior. At its heart, ableism is rooted in the assumption that disabled people require 'fixing' and defines people by their disability. Like racism and sexism, ableism classifies entire groups of people as 'less than' and includes harmful stereotypes, misconceptions and generalisations of people with disabilities.*

For example, mocking or dismissing someone with a disability or thinking disabilities are only visible (blind, missing a limb) is being ableist.

In Australia, the Disability Discrimination Act 1992 outlines what a disability is and the types. Covered under the act are physical disability, intellectual disability, mental illness, sensory disability, neurological disability, immunological disability, learning disability and physical disfigurement. Any impairment or condition that falls into these categories to be classified as a disability must affect the person's ability to take care of their daily activities and must have persisted or is likely to persist for more than six months.

If we think about our world, it wasn't built for people with disability so, because of that, the world is inherently 'ableist' — made for able-bodied people.

Healthline.com gives a good list of ableist examples (prejudices and discrimination):

- believing people with disability have less value or worth
- assuming people with disability want to be 'healed' or can simply 'overcome' their disability
- suggesting they're 'inspirational' for handling everyday activities and routine tasks
- assuming they lead an unhappy, limited life
- assuming they can't do things for themselves
- using words like 'normal' and 'healthy' to describe non-disabled people
- asking intrusive questions about someone's disability
- touching someone or any equipment or devices they use without permission
- ignoring requests for accommodations or refusing to acknowledge someone's disability
- refusing to use the terms someone requests like 'deaf person', 'neurodivergent' or 'wheelchair user'
- using ableist language, especially after someone asks you to stop

Other examples are building inaccessible buildings (no ramps) or street signs (no braille), casting an able-bodied actor as a disabled person, making a movie without audio descriptions, choosing an inaccessible building for a meeting, using the disabled bathroom when you're not disabled, talking baby talk or talking slower to a person who is intellectually disabled or using phrases like 'You're a retard', 'She's such a psycho', 'Are you off your meds?', or, 'I don't even think of you as disabled'.

Many people who are ableist do so in good will. They don't even know they are being ableist. For example, the people who grab me and want to help me off the train, even when I tell them I'm okay, are actually being ableist. In their mind, they're being a good Samaritan. Or my youngest's Guidance Officer who, in Year 3, slid enrolment papers across the desk at my husband and me for the segregated special school down the road and told us that her IQ entitled her to go there. The GO added, 'She could be a leader there.' My sharp reply was, 'No, she's staying here (in mainstream) and why can't she be a leader here?' This was blatant ableism. The underlying message was that my daughter, because of her Down syndrome, was not intelligent enough to keep attending the regular school and she could never be a leader. She wasn't worthy of being there in the schooling system made for able-bodied children. This was just one example of many I could give concerning my daughter's journey through mainstream education. And I am proud to say she was on the Public Relations Committee in Year 6 so she became a leader in her mainstream school!

Other people are said to be ableist because they have a fear of disability, they are uncertain how to behave around people with disability, they haven't been educated on how to help people with disability or they have learnt attitudes from parents, the media, their culture or religion.

Society obviously has a lot to answer for and, unless these prejudices and discriminatory practices are called out, they will continue.

What can you do about discrimination? If the discrimination occurs at work, the Fair Work Commission in Australia states that employees and potential employees are protected from discrimination at work under the Fair Work Act. Employers who take harmful ('adverse') action because of discrimination may break general protection laws.

An employer may break general protection laws if they:

- dismiss an employee **because of** their features or attributes
- don't hire someone **because of** their features or attributes
- treat a person differently to others **because of** their features or attributes
- offer an employee worse terms than other employees **because of** their features or attributes
- don't give a worker their legal entitlements **because of** their features or attributes
- change an employee's job in a way that has a negative effect **because of** their features or attributes
- take or threaten to take adverse action to force an employee to do something **because of** their features or attributes

The Fair Work Commission has the power to deal with these issues.

If you believe you are being discriminated against, there are some things you can do:

- Start with a conversation. Speak to the individual and tell them how you feel.
- Build a strong network of supportive family and friends around you.
- If it's at work, speak to your employer. Do this as it's possible the individual involved doesn't realise they're being discriminatory and have prejudices.
- If the behaviour continues, you may choose to take things further. You may want to go to the Fair Work

Ombudsman, the Human Rights Commission, seek advice from a lawyer etc. Of course, this all depends on where it's occurring. You may even want to contact your local MP and call out the prejudice and discrimination you're seeing in the wider community.

Again, I'm not a lawyer so I'm not giving you legal advice. I have provided the above information to ensure you understand what prejudice and discrimination is so you can lead your best life. All people deserve to be living in victory.

∞∞∞∞

This chapter was heavy … but it dealt with issues close to my heart and which have affected my life. To lead our best life by being victorious, there are things we can do like taking control of the direction of our life—by goal setting, staying away from toxic relationships and being educated on what prejudice and discrimination are.

In Chapter 4, we'll look at ways we can be weirdly wonderfully present in our day-to-day life.

Chapter 4 - Be *Weirdly Wonderfully Present*

'The art of life is to live in the present moment.'—Emmet Fox

'Therefore do not worry about tomorrow, for tomorrow will worry about itself. Each day has enough trouble of its own.'—Matthew 6:34

∞∞∞∞

Have you heard the saying, *'Yesterday is history, tomorrow is a mystery, today is a gift of God, which is why we call it the present?'*

In this chapter, I want to focus on a mindset that I try to engage every day.

This mindset is, *'What is happening now?'*

With my overactive mind, which wants to worry, be anxious or depressed, bring up the past and push me into the future, this question has helped me to enjoy and lead my best life.

I have found focusing on this question and concentrating on what's happening now, at this present moment, can be exciting and pleasurable, giving me the warm fuzzies. It opens me up to taking on new opportunities and making calculated risks. It provides me with the space to make important decisions and to jump into new projects on the spur of the moment. Living in the present gives me a sense of appreciation for the people around me and where I am at. Do you live in the present as much as possible?

I learnt this mindset from a yoga teacher. Her frequent question was, *'What is the most important time on your watch?'* The answer is, of course, 'NOW.' This made me think about what I do—and I realised that I wasn't focusing enough on the present. I was way too often reliving the past or cast into the future … so I changed my mindset.

During my research, I found the following quote from Tolstoy. He agrees!

∞∞∞∞

'There is only one time that is important – NOW! It is the most important time because it is the only time that we have any power.'—Leo Tolstoy

∞∞∞∞

Let's look at twelve practical ways that you, too, can be present each day.

Stop the worrying

I used to be a worrier. I would worry about everything and anything—but did it help? It may have, occasionally, but it usually just sucked me away from the present moment, raised my blood pressure, churned my guts and gave me a headache!

When you worry, you're extremely concerned about something—and sometimes that's warranted. If you had a 'who gives a damn' attitude all the time, the results could be catastrophic. For example, if you weren't worried about keeping to your budget and splashed out on all the things you liked at the sales then, when your household bills came due, you probably wouldn't have the money to pay them. If overspending led you to not having the money to pay for your groceries, your rent or mortgage, your electricity or your medicines then you're going to be in real trouble.

When I look back over my life, I can pinpoint stages where worry consumed me to the point that my anxiety was a shark on steroids. And when I reflect more on those times, I can remember clearly the physical, emotional and psychological effects the worrying had on me. I categorically wasn't leading my best life!

Research has shown the amount people worry is actually related to their genes, parents and other role models, and personal mindsets—the nature-nurture influence. Did you know you can be genetically more prone to worry, just as you can be more prone to addictions or mental illness?

Research has found that 85% of what people worry about never happens. That obviously means that 15% does happen—but it also shows that people spend a lot of time worrying for no good reason.

There can be negative effects for people who often worry. Worrying can:

- interfere with your life
- stop you from concentrating on what you're doing
- stop you from doing things
- stop you from relaxing
- increase anxiety

To put it simply, worrying prevents you from being in the present moment and leading your best life … and that's not what we want.

If you think about your family and friends, you'll be able to identify people who worry more, others who worry sometimes and others who seem to not worry about anything. You will know of people who focus on the worst-case scenario which feeds their worry.

Much of my worrying over the past twenty years has been related to finances and my children. I was the breadwinner and the one who looked after the budget—and there were times I worried about not being able to buy groceries or pay the mortgage. The worst-case scenario I could see, of losing our house, was a raging bull with flaring nostrils. This worst-case scenario exacerbated my worry. I remember when part of our roof fell off and an inspection showed the whole roof needed repairing and repainting. I remember crying at the salesman and asking him for the lowest price possible and for a finance plan to pay for it.

As a parent of children with medical needs, I would worry when they were on camp. My nails would be bitten down to the quick. I had to remind myself that I'd be phoned if anything happened but my worrying didn't settle until they returned home.

Worrying about my finances and making sure we had money was healthy but worrying about my children when they were at camp didn't serve any useful purpose.

It's likely you worry because you don't know how to fix or change something or because you don't know how something is going to turn out. Or maybe you do know what an outcome will be and you know it's going to be unpleasant. Or maybe you just think the outcome is going to be unpleasant (though it may not be).

Research shows that people often worry because they're trying to distract themselves from other emotions or solving the issue. Instead of worrying, research has found the best strategy is to problem-solve the situation. (If you're a nail-biter like me, your nails can become lovely and long … which is a good thing, isn't it?)

Let's look at what problem-solving involves:

- First, you must evaluate your situation (maybe getting someone else's help if you're highly emotional). To evaluate your situation, look at the issue from all angles—methodically and without emotion. After this, you can either verbalise or write down what the problem is.

- By evaluating the situation and identifying the problem, pinpoint what has caused or is causing it. You may find just one or multiple factors. Take time with this part, as the root cause might not be the first one you think of. A good strategy is to list these down.

- The next step is to come up with potential solutions. Brainstorm to find as many solutions as you can. Again, write them down.

- Next, formulate a plan from this list of possible solutions. When choosing the best solution, the one

that eliminates the problem will be the ideal one. Depending on what the problem is, you may need a multi-step plan.
- Once your plan is formulated, put it into action. Action, not worrying, is the aim.
- The final step is to evaluate the result of actioning the plan. If it solved the problem, that's great! If not, you may need to go through the process again using different potential solutions.

For example, here's an illustration of this process for a woman who's just lost her job and she's worried about her finances.
- Katie could sit and worry and worry and worry—but that's not going to solve the problem.
- She knows the problem—she lost her job and needs another one ASAP.
- Instead of worrying, Katie thinks about what caused her to lose her job. It may have been the company's loss of sales but it may also have been her constant late arrival.
- She brainstorms what she can do. If she doesn't have a budget, she could write one. She could cut back on takeaways or streaming services or nonessentials. She could update her resume and register with a job provider. She could think about who she knows with contacts. She could door-knock or think about any skills she could hire out.
- Once Katie lists potential solutions, she can decide what she's going to do. The first step might be to contact the bank about her mortgage and discuss options. The second step might be to cancel all her paid

streaming services for the moment. The next may be to register for welfare etc.

- After these steps are undertaken and she has applied for new jobs or decided to study something else, the final step is to evaluate the position she's now in. (If Katie has faith, she should remember to give her situation to God and trust that it will turn out how it's meant to—which she may or may not like.)
- If necessary, Katie may need to go back to the brainstorming stage for some new ideas.

To summarise, worrying steals our joy, can make us sick and prevents us from living in the present and leading our best life. Problem-solving will help.

Don't live in the past

Some people don't focus on the present or the future but instead they focus on the past. The past may be full of regrets and wishing they'd made different choices … or the past may be a time where life was happier and they imagine being back there.

Memories, both good and bad, are to be remembered— there is no other reason why our brains would retain them and bring them to the front of our mind. Being honest, a memory of something in my past pops into my head every day—sometimes they are good memories and sometimes they aren't. Most people would experience this.

Looking to the past can become dangerous if you stay stuck there. Whether you're remembering your past as good or bad, being stuck in the past robs you of the time you have now.

If your focus on the past is the rehashing of your mistakes or things you wished you'd never done then that needs to stop. I'm a rehasher and stopping this is something I've had to consciously do.

If you're a rehasher, you must internalise the fact that being human means that you make mistakes and your decisions don't always have the desired outcomes or great outcomes.
(For more on this, see 'Learn from your mistakes, they don't define you' in Chapter 2)

We make decisions for a multitude of reasons. Our maturity level, current circumstances and psyche all influence the decisions we make. We can't see into the future (bring me a TARDIS!) and, if we could, many of our decisions we make would probably be different.

When we look back, we're seeing things after the event. Hindsight allows us to see what went wrong. We may regret our decision but, at the time we made it, we thought it was the right one. Be kind to yourself!

For our mental health and peace of mind, we need to change how we look at our past. Instead of beating ourselves up about our decisions and how they turned out, we need to find the lesson and learn from it. We should also try to identify any blessings that came from the experience.

By finding the lessons and the blessings from our past, we are being kind to ourselves. What are your lessons and blessings? (If past negative triggers are affecting you, go to the Book and Bookshelf metaphor in Chapter 6 *Be Weirdly Wonderfully Resilient*.)

Don't let yesterday use up too much of today.

Find the beauty in everyday things

Everyone has heard the saying, 'Stop and smell the roses', meaning to live in the present and be in the moment. But it can mean to literally stop and smell the roses. Flowers, trees and shrubs are beautiful. You may be amazed to find how much more relaxed you can feel after spending time at a botanical garden, in a forest, at a creek, stopping to look at the flowers in a shop or wandering around your neighbourhood to see what's growing in local gardens. I have a particular fascination with fungi … and I get a burst of happiness when I'm bushwalking with my partner and he spots some to show me.

As a person living with low vision, I don't take for granted what I can see. I have friends who are fully blind — some from birth and others who've lost their sight over time. Many of those who lost their sight over time particularly struggle with not being able to see their loved one's faces anymore. With the full loss of their vision, they must rely on touch or their visual memory (what they remember from when they could see). Don't take your vision for granted.

Beauty in your everyday life does not have to be physical. It can also be the experiences that bring you simple pleasures. It can be the enjoyment of sleeping in on your day off, the conversation you have with a friend you bump into at the shops, watching ducks swim at the local park or watching your favourite movie.

As I get older, I'm finding it's those little things that bring me daily pleasure and keep me in the present.

Slow down and enjoy life. See the beauty around you … the golden sunset, the intricate spider's web, the glistening dew drops…

Do one thing at a time

Women like to say they're good at multitasking, which is now often referred to as switchtasking. Dave Crenshaw has explained that multitasking is actually switchtasking—which makes perfect sense because the person is quickly switching back and forth between two or more tasks.

Do you think women are able to switchtask successfully?

It's interesting that the evidence for switchtasking has said that switchtasking doesn't really work. Why? Because the person is being less efficient and achieving less. The cost of switchtasking is the transition time of mental effort and the energy it takes to go from one task to the other.

Do you agree?

The research, and my own opinion from personal experience, shows that it's much more efficient to start and finish one task at a time.

I am a list maker. Maybe you are too. I write down in my diary what I plan to get done during the day and what activities and appointments are on. I also have categorised 'to do' lists at the back of my diary—categories such as home, author, pottery and volunteering. I smile and feel satisfied when I'm able to tick things off.

When I think of all the tasks I do, I know I can only really do one task at a time. If I try to undertake multiple tasks, one typically gets left undone. A good example is if I'm cooking and trying to pay bills, I'll forget that I'm cooking which doesn't have good consequences—usually a burned dinner! My brain only focuses well when I'm doing one thing. Once that's done, I can move on to the next task. Even if I cut a job in half, such as the washing, I still need to remember later that I need to hang it out—and I'm good at forgetting! It's so easy to forget but my list in my diary helps me there. Other strategies I've found that work for me are to set an alarm on my phone or write a word on my hand.

If you're doing one thing at a time, you're more likely to be in the present.

Limit your distractions

Who doesn't love a good distraction? Distractions are particularly useful when we're procrastinating—but can be annoying when we're trying to stay on task. How often does a ping or notification on your phone tempt you or take you away from your work? How often do you go to do one task and end up doing a different one?

Simply put, the easiest way to limit distractions is to remove them. Here are some examples but I'm sure you can think of others as well:

- take Facebook or Instagram off your computer or phone
- put your phone on silent
- block out chunks of time in your diary where you'll attend to particular jobs or activities
- decide that you'll get a specific task done before you go onto another one
- set an alarm so you're not distracted by what time it is

I have a structured week with set activities on most days. This structure helps my anxiety and limits my distractions. Of course, there are times when changes occur and I have to deal with those. During my planning, I always make sure I've factored in 'me time'. 'Me time' could be exercise, a nap, playing with clay, going to the beach etc.

While I'm having my 'me time', I try to avoid looking at my phone or answering it. My aim is to be fully present and focused.

Have a ritual each day that you really enjoy

Some days you are so busy that you don't have time to stop for two minutes. You get up and, before you know it, you're falling exhausted back into bed. The day may even be a blur in your mind. The next day, this is repeated. The next day, this is repeated. And soon, you may even say, 'Where did that week go?' You may think you were present in each moment but, in reality, you weren't. Your mind was elsewhere or stressed or full of random thoughts.

To bring you back more into the present, another strategy could be to take the time to do something each day that you enjoy (that does not include eating or drinking alcohol). This could be walking the dog, listening to a podcast, watching your favourite TV show, reading to the kids, journaling your thoughts or listening to music while you're in the shower. This activity is something that will feed your good mental health and can take your mind off your worries and the stresses of everyday life. One of the things I do each day is to listen to a Bible devotion in the morning. This helps start my day by remembering that God is in control. And before I go to sleep, I like to read a book and pray. What could you do or what do you do?

Spend time away from your phone

Don't you hate it when you go out and accidentally leave your phone at home? On the rare occasion I've done this, it felt as if an arm was missing. It was a strange feeling and, to be honest, I didn't like it!

Social media sucks you in, games suck you in and streaming services suck you in. I know what it's like trying to take screens away from children and teens—it's as though they're being put in a dungeon or about to be executed or some other dreadful thing. They hate it.

If you're trying to spend less time on your devices, putting them on silent is one way. If you need to be contacted then tuck the phone in your pocket. I had an incident where my phone was in my bag on silent while I was at a conference and I didn't check it until afternoon tea. Upon checking my messages, I found multiple calls from school telling me my daughter's support worker hadn't turned up to take her home. Of course, I freaked out! Thankfully, my daughter was safe in the office and the support worker had arrived by the time I rang back. This was a big lesson!

Another strategy could be to put the device on charge a few metres away from you ... where you can still hear it ring but you must get up to answer it.

Have you got any other ideas?

In summary, to be fully present and leading our best lives, we need to think about our phone usage and limit it as much as we can.

Question limiting beliefs

Essentially, limiting beliefs are the assumptions we make about ourselves which are paired with our beliefs about the world we live in. Basically, they are negative mindsets. These beliefs form over many years from our family, education, life experiences and societal influences. And the worst part about these negative mindsets is that they can prevent us from achieving new things, challenging ourselves, going out in the world, applying for our dream job and maybe even doing the activities that we really want to try. They will stop us from leading our best life … so they must go!

Three examples of limiting beliefs are:

- I'm no good at maths.
- I can't make friends.
- I will never get married.

∞∞∞∞

'Life has no limitations, except the ones you make.'—Les Brown

∞∞∞∞

The danger with limiting beliefs is that we can reinforce the belief by making it come true. For example, a limiting belief might be, 'I hate going to parties as no one will talk to me … but it's my friend's 21st so I really should go.' I go to the party, sit in the corner all night and no one talks to me. The next morning, I think about the party and my limiting belief has just been reinforced. The next time there's a party, I'll most likely repeat the thinking that no one will talk to me—so I probably won't go to avoid the disappointment.

This reinforcement of the limiting belief can also be called a *self-fulfilling prophecy*. A self-fulfilling prophecy is when you believe something and then make it happen, either consciously or subconsciously. This self-fulfilling prophecy then reinforces itself and makes the limiting belief stronger. In the above example, no one could have talked to me because I was hidden away in another room or I had a scowl on my face or I made a sarcastic comment or I spent the night with my nose in my phone… My behaviour stopped people from wanting to talk to me.

Another example of limiting beliefs could be where a guy has been receiving rejections to go out on a date. He sees a girl he would like to ask out but thinks, 'She's probably going to reject me, too.' He goes up to her with his head bowed and mumbles, 'You probably don't want to go out with me but I thought I would ask you anyway.' He stares at his shoes. The girl, who doesn't know him, obviously says, 'No thanks.' This rejection reaffirms his beliefs. If he had gone up to her confidently and smiled, there is no guarantee but far more chance she may have said, 'Yes'. You can easily see the difference and how limiting beliefs and self-fulfilling prophecies are detrimental.

Limiting beliefs can stop us from being present because they change how we're feeling and reacting to an event which we could be enjoying. It would be terrible if our once-in-a-lifetime opportunity came but, because of our limiting belief, we didn't take it.

The best way to address limiting beliefs is to challenge and reframe them. Sometimes you can challenge a limiting belief and it will still come true. I stopped having birthday parties because I was so upset by what I perceived as rejection from invitees who said they could not attend or who said they would attend and didn't. Of course, when I challenged the limiting belief and did hold a party, there were many responses of, 'I can't come sorry because I'm doing this…' My immediate thought was, 'I'm not good enough for them to want to come to my party', which just wasn't true at all. I had to really work on reframing this limiting belief to, 'I'm going to have a great time at my party no matter who comes. Those who want to come and can come will come. Whether it is one or fifty, it doesn't matter.'

Practise mindfulness

I want to spend a bit of time talking about mindfulness. Being mindful has really helped me to be less anxious and to stay in the present—and it can help you.

So, what is mindfulness?

Mindfulness is intentionally being in control of your mind rather than letting your mind be in control of you. When you are mindful, you pay attention to the present moment. You are aware of what's taking place right now and using all your senses—sight, hearing, touch, taste, smell—in the experience.

Mindfulness brings us instantly into the present and can help us cope with everyday life and deal with tough times. It can also aid in relaxation and increase productivity.

How does mindfulness work?

When you're being mindful, your mind is used in two different ways:

- The *opened mind*, where you're aware of the present moment. You know what you're thinking, what emotions you're experiencing and your physical sensations. When you're in this state, you don't judge what you're thinking or feeling and you don't try to change them.
- The *focused mind*, where you stay focused on one thing at a time like eating your dinner slowly and really tasting the flavours and feeling the texture of the food in your mouth.

Live the actual moment, as only this moment is life.

Here are five ways you can be mindful:

Focus only on the present moment. The key to mindfulness is focusing only on the present moment. To do this, you can ask yourself some questions such as:
- What is happening right now?
- Is my breathing slow or fast?
- Am I tired?
- Am I hungry?
- Am I angry?
- Am I hot?
- Is my back sore?

When asking yourself the questions, use your five senses—see, hear, taste, touch and smell. Other thoughts may want to intrude and take you away from the present. If so, let them come and go as if they were moving on a conveyor belt.

Concentrate on what's happening around you. This will also stop your intruding thoughts. To concentrate on what's happening around you, ask yourself:
- What sounds can I hear?
- What can I smell?
- What are people doing around me?
- How are people around me acting?

When you're answering these questions, concentrate only on the facts and don't try to interpret what's going on. For example, if I saw a child stomping their feet, I could interpret that as they're angry. When being mindful, I'd observe that the child was stomping their feet and there's a clomping sound … and that is all.

Don't make judgements about anything you notice. When being mindful, you're sticking to the facts of what's happening, just like in the child stomping example. You aren't labelling things as 'good' or 'bad' or making any other judgements about what you see or hear. You're just noticing things around you. For example, instead of labelling a particular smell as 'bad', just notice the smell without judging it… It smells like rotting fish.

Try mindful breathing. To do mindful breathing, sit quietly with your eyes either open or closed and focus on your breath. While you breathe from your diaphragm, ask yourself:
- What does my breathing feel like?
- What does it sound like?
- Where do I first feel the breath in my body?

Try mindful meditation. Some people like to meditate. It's the same as mindful breathing—you close your eyes and focus on your breathing and then quietly repeat a word or phrase. During the meditation, allow your thoughts to come and go and try not to follow them. When your thoughts on other things come, gently bring your mind back to your breathing.

When I do mindful breathing, I often find that other thoughts will intrude. To stop these, I visualise a stop sign. I park the thought at the stop sign and tell the thought, 'I'll come back to you later.' This clears my mind so I can be present in the moment again. You may find a different strategy that will work for you. Just remember, the aim is for calmness and tranquillity in your body and mind.

Another type of mindfulness—be mindful of where you are. With my long cane, I get stared at and pointed at wherever I go and I often feel vulnerable. My cane tells the world that I cannot see well so I feel that I could be 'easy pickings' for unscrupulous people.

Because I'm acutely aware of my vulnerability as a disabled person, I'm mindful of what type of bag I use—either a cross over handbag or a backpack. I'm also mindful of where I set them down—usually in my lap or under a chair leg so they are harder to snatch. I don't wear earphones or listen to anything when I'm out, even when sitting on the train, because I don't want to be distracted or unable to hear. It's important that I listen and use my other senses to inform me of what's going on around me.

In the past, I would tend to look down when walking to avoid eye contact with people. But I now force myself to make eye contact. I want people to know that I have some eyesight and I feel that eye contact makes me less of a potential victim. I have also learnt some self-defence moves and I attend the gym to become strong. When out at night time I don't catch public transport or go to out-of-the-way places on my own. I would love to trust the world and say, 'I'll never be a victim of crime', but reality says otherwise.

If you're living with a disability or difference that makes you vulnerable, your safety is something that you must be mindful of.

Always be aware of your surroundings.

Be grateful

Dictionary.com says that *having gratitude is to be warmly or deeply appreciative of kindness or benefits received; thankful.*

I would love for you to stop reading and take a moment to think of three things that you're grateful or thankful for. They could be the roof over your head, food in your tummy, your job, your children, the lovely weather or even just for having the time to read my book!

∞∞∞∞

'Cultivate the habit of being grateful for every good thing that comes to you, and to give thanks continuously. And because all things have contributed to your advancement, you should include all things in your gratitude.' — Ralph Waldo Emerson

∞∞∞∞

There's a lot of research which confirms that gratitude is very beneficial to your mind, keeps you in the present and grounded.

Here's an overview of some recent psychological findings related to the study of gratitude:
- People who express their gratitude for each other tend to be more willing to forgive others, are less self-centred and have stronger relationships.
- Showing gratitude makes us more optimistic about life.
- Being grateful improves both mental and physical health and well-being.
- Gratitude reduces stress levels.
- Gratitude can help people to make better long-term decisions about their lives.

Consider this quote from the Wall Street Journal's article 'Thank you, No, Thank you.'

'... adults who feel grateful have more energy, more optimism, more social connections and more happiness than those who do not, according to studies conducted over the past decade. They're also less likely to be depressed, envious, greedy or alcoholics.' —Melinda Beck

If you haven't thought much about showing gratitude, here are some ideas to start with:

- For a friend or someone you're in a relationship with, you could write a letter, a card, or an email; film a video, write a song or a poem and tell the person why you are grateful for them being in your life. You could also bake something for them, do something special for them or give them a gift.

- Another thing you can do is start a gratitude journal. A gratitude journal involves spending some time in the morning, or just before you go to bed, thinking about the day and the things and people in your life for which you are grateful. Write them down in the notebook and your brain's negative thoughts will change to positive over time. This is particularly good for people who have anxiety or depression. I remember a time, back when I was teaching and stressed out, a colleague said to me that every day she looked for one good thing that had happened. This attitude really helped me as my head was flip-flopping into negative mindsets. I was much happier as I reflected on a child's smile, a kind word, a child who helped me, a child who followed my directions, a lesson that went well, nice weather or that I got a break to eat my lunch.

- For Christians, saying grace and prayers gives you the opportunity to thank God for all the good people, things and opportunities in your life, and time to praise Him for who He is. You shouldn't just be making requests to God. My gratitude journal is also my prayer journal where, before I write anything else, I thank God for the good things that have happened that day. You need to always remember that God is good and showers you with blessings—though sometimes you need to stop and think to realise what your blessings are.

- Instead of or in addition to a gratitude journal, you can keep a gratitude jar. All you need is a bottle or small container, paper and a pen. On the paper, write down what you are grateful for and pop it in the jar. Ideally, do this each day but at least on a regular basis. On New Year's Eve, open the jar and read them—and you'll be surprised by how many blessings you received. And, of course, you don't have to wait until New Year's Eve. If you're having a tough day or negative mindsets have taken root, read the notes. They will help give you courage, strength, hope and optimism to keep going. You'll see your blessings in messages to yourself in black and white—or whatever colour pen and paper you use!

Are you thankful for the air you breathe, the food that nourishes you, the home you live in, the sunshine that brightens up your day or your pet who adores you? Are you grateful for the help you receive, the medical services or equipment you use or the NDIS?

Every little detail in your life counts.

Appreciate the little things

I think I started learning to appreciate the little things when Maeve started having craniofacial surgeries. In her second skull reconstruction, the dura surrounding her brain tore and she suffered a major bleed. We only knew something was wrong when the nurse came out ashen-faced to say there had been an issue but everything was okay. We didn't know what had occurred but we learnt later that she nearly died. The junior doctor told us he'd never seen that much blood before.

When Maeve was three years old, she needed another skull reconstruction and a shunt inserted in her brain for hydrocephalus—too much cerebrospinal fluid (CSF) in the brain. During this surgery, the neurosurgeon physically pushed her brain back down into her head because it was bulging out of a weak section of her skull. The neurosurgeon gravely told us in PICU that she would most likely never walk again. We prayed and I thank God that she can walk.

These events and others have caused me to see life in a different way.

My youngest daughter's intellectual disability has meant that she takes longer to learn things—from her developmental milestones, to learning to swim fast enough to go to Special Olympics National Titles, to being semi-independent. She has needed a lot of purposeful teaching and practice. She hasn't picked up the many things my other children picked up instinctively and this has made me appreciate the little things in life.

My dog going crazy when I open the front door or snuggling up to me when I'm on the couch fills my heart with happiness. Sitting on the back balcony with my partner.

Listening to the magpies singing in the rain and the lorrikeets tweeting as they fly overhead towards their nightly roost. These things, and many others, are priceless. I'm grateful for them. What little things do you appreciate?

Name and manage your emotions

Every moment of the day you are experiencing an emotion and, if you're living in the present, it won't be hard for you to be able to identify what your emotion is and what is causing it.

When I think of emotions, the children's movie Inside Out by Pixar comes to mind. My youngest and I loved the movie so much that I purchased the character dolls. If you don't know the movie, it's about a pre-teen girl named Riley who moves to the city and is unhappy. Inside her head are five emotions, represented by animated characters. Joy, Sadness, Fear, Anger and Disgust. In the movie, the emotions all work to guide and protect Riley when the family moves house. As with many movies, there are ups and downs and a happy ending.

After watching Inside Out, Jessica, who was young at the time, would often touch her forehead and say, 'I'm putting joy in my head.' After she'd dried her tears, she'd smile and say, 'Joy is in my head now!' This always struck me as a good strategy because I think there are times when we need to deliberately and consciously change our emotions and choose to feel more positive.

How do you manage your emotions?

Research has shown that we don't have to let our emotions rule or control us ... so let's look at some strategies for managing them:

- First, take the time to name the emotion we are experiencing. For example, when my hands are shaking or I'm sitting on the toilet with an upset stomach, I'm consciously aware that I'm experiencing anxiety and I'm scared.
- Then acknowledge why we're feeling that way. For example, I'm anxious because I must give a speech and I hate public speaking.
- Next, think logically about the situation and answer this question, 'Is what the emotion telling me accurate?' If I'm in the forest being chased by a bear then I can be sure the emotion of fear is accurate! If my fear is about public speaking then it's probably not.
- Finally, to manage the emotion, we focus on what we're trying to do and why we're trying to do it. For example, I'm giving the speech to raise awareness of a cause I'm passionate about.

People often bottle up negative emotions but psychologist Susan David Bottling advises this isn't an effective management technique. Why do you think it isn't effective? She says if we try to avoid the situation and the emotion then these situations and emotions will always stay the same … and be negative. To lead our best life, we want our emotions to be positive. No more bottling up!

When I think of managing my emotions and reactions, I can't help but remember some wise words from a deputy principal when I was complaining about disrespect towards me. She told me I was *choosing* to let poor student behaviour affect me. I didn't have to get upset or angry. I could let it wash over me. This comment made me stop and think and change how I managed my emotions.

Always remember, your goal is to have your emotions work for you, not against you.

One final gem of wisdom … *Holding unforgiveness, bitterness and anger towards someone is like drinking poison. It won't necessarily affect them but it will definitely affect your health.*

Have a passion or hobby

I have already shared some guidance about following and developing our hobbies, passions and talents in Chapter 2 so I'm not going to add a lot more here … except to say that when I'm engrossed in my writing or pottery, I'm in the present. I'm not thinking about anything else but the words on the page or the clay spinning on the wheel.

In my twenties, my hobbies were canoeing and sailing and these made me feel free. Being out in nature and ripping through waves with the wind in my hair was so good.

The passions you follow can be almost anything—as long as they're legal, don't hurt other people or yourself and you can afford them. If you don't already have a passion or you haven't yet found something you really enjoy doing, you should consider finding one. In addition to keeping you in the present, hobbies and passions can lead to new relationships and connections with other people. They can give you an identity beyond just being a parent or a carer or being your work title. You may even find that you're able to turn your passion into a source of income and a career.

∞∞∞∞

In this chapter, I've shared twelve practical ways to be present. We've explored the issue of worrying and how to live in the present and find beauty in everyday things. We've examined the importance of doing one thing at a time and limiting distractions and the need for an enjoyable ritual each day and how to spend time away from our phones. We've questioned those limiting beliefs, looked at ways to practise mindfulness, being grateful and stopping to appreciate the little things. Finally, we examined choosing and managing our emotions and the benefits of having a passion or hobby.

In Chapter 5, I'll share some thoughts about being weirdly wonderfully balanced.

Chapter 5 - Be *Weirdly Wonderfully Balanced*

'Balance is not something you find, it's something you create.'—Jana Kingsford

'There is an appointed time for everything and there is a time for every event under heaven. A time to give birth and a time to die. A time to plant and a time to uproot what is planted. A time to kill and a time to heal. A time to tear down and a time to build up. A time to weep and a time to laugh. A time to mourn and a time to dance. A time to throw stones and a time to gather stones. A time to embrace and a time to shun embracing. A time to search and a time to give up as lost. A time to keep and a time to throw away. A time to tear apart and a time to sew together. A time to be silent and a time to speak. A time to love and a time to hate. A time for war and a time for peace.'—Ecclesiastes 3:1-8

∞∞∞∞

Have you ever felt out-of-control? Like you want time to stop so you can catch up? Or maybe you've been sick for a long time and you know it's related to stress. I have. I think this chapter is important because you can't be the best version of yourself or come into your greatness and lead your best life if you're unbalanced. Come with me now as we look at balancing your mind, your time, your finances, your social life, maintaining self-care and setting boundaries.

A survey conducted in 2017 by Medibank, the Australian health fund, reported that five million Australians were suffering from stress, commonly due to lack of sleep, work pressures and social media. Seven years on, this number would be even higher. That's a lot of people! Wherever you are in the world, I'm sure you can identify with this.

In the last two years of my teaching career, I was constantly at the doctors. I caught multiple viruses and infections, I had daily diarrhoea, I kept breaking out in staph infections all over my skin and I was constantly covered in hives. Why? In one word, BURNOUT. I was feeling so stressed out, overwhelmed with life and anxious that my immunity was low, leading to constant sickness.

My life was unbalanced.

Once I left teaching, the majority of the physical symptoms disappeared. This surprised me, though it shouldn't have.

What I learnt from my breakdown was important—I can't always control the circumstances that life throws my way but

I *can* control how well I take care of myself and the strategies I put in place to cope with the amount of stress I feel.

I'm sure that you'll agree that when you're too tired, eating poorly or generally run-down, you're more reactive to stressful situations. You may even create more problems for yourself because of your short temper. It's hard to stay calm when you're unbalanced!

I have red flags and a pattern of behaviour that tells me I'm unbalanced—and I can tell you exactly what they are:

1. A short temper
2. Negative thoughts about life and my self-worth
3. Tears
4. Suicidal thoughts.

Psychology tells us that some stress is beneficial for us. A manageable amount of stress can keep us safe, generate energy and improve alertness, motivation and performance. Manageable stress can also improve our memory through the growth of stem cells that become brain cells. The problem with stress, as I've already alluded to with my situation, occurs when there is too much. Too much stress causes negative effects on our body and mind.

I'm sure you can think of some negative effects of stress … but I did some research and put together the following list:

- reflux, hyperacidity, heartburn, oesophageal inflammation
- irritable bowel syndrome
- ulcers
- diarrhoea and constipation
- indigestion
- high blood pressure
- heart disease

- stroke
- bladder infection
- high cholesterol
- immune system related disorders
- asthma
- allergies and skin diseases
- colds and infections
- muscle spasms and muscle pains
- motility disturbance
- cancer
- neurodegenerative disorders
- fatigue
- anxiety
- depression
- insomnia
- alcohol and drug misuse and dependence
- concentration and memory problems

These aren't good, I'm sure you'll agree! But the good news is that stress can be reduced or managed. Let's now look at some ways.

The end goal of managing stress will be you're leading your best life.

Your whole of life

In the late 1990s when I had separated from my first husband and was in my black hole of depression, my deputy principal at the time gave me a metaphor about being balanced. It made so much sense to me at the time that it has stayed with me. To put it simply, to stay in balance, you need to be like a chair—all four legs firmly planted on the floor. The legs of the chair represent spirituality, health, relationships and career—and if one of those legs becomes wobbly or breaks, you'll fall over. At the time, my health and relationship legs of the chair were poor so I had fallen over. When my mental health improved and I'd moved on from my marriage, the legs became stable and my life felt balanced.

I recently attended a seminar with Dr Carolyn Russell. She spoke about the areas of our life that need to be in balance for us to be happy and healthy. I liked what she shared so I'm sharing it with you. This is a practical activity—you'll need a pen and a piece of paper.

First, draw five circles, one within the other, like the diagram below. Label each of the circles as shown, starting from the outside: Social, Physical, Mind, Heart, Centre.

We're going to start from the outside circle, which is the social circle, then work our way to the centre circle.

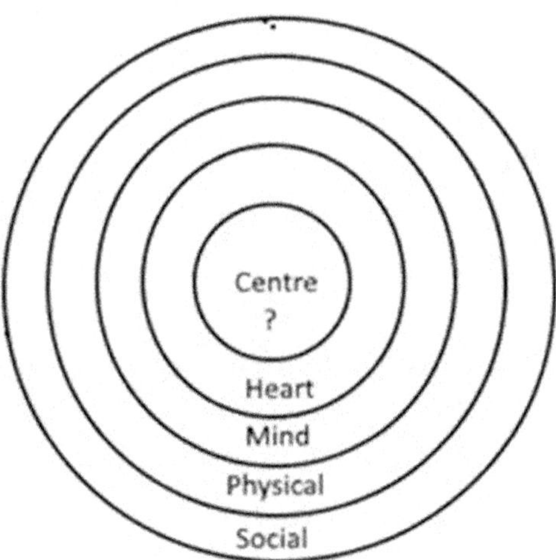

Social Circle (outside circle): These are your friends you know well and share intimately with. These are the people who make you feel known and loved and who share the joys and challenges of life with you. Research has shown that married people generally need two to three people who are close, apart from their partner. Single people need five to six close friends. They can be in person, on the phone or over the Internet. Who are yours?

- Write them on your diagram.
- Do you think you have enough or too many friends?

Physical Circle: This is how you look after our physical body. This includes the amount of exercise you do, healthy or unhealthy eating and the amount of sleep you get.

- Do you look after your physical body?
- Write down what you do—how much do you exercise, do you eat a balanced diet and do you get enough sleep?

Mind Circle: This refers to your thinking patterns and whether you mainly have positive or negative thinking. Mental illnesses would be included here as well.

- Are you looking after your mental health or are you stressed, anxious, depressed etc?
- Write down how you feel your mind is and how you're looking after it.

Heart Circle: This is your self-identity and self-esteem and how you feel about yourself. Your heart circle could be negative or positive.

- How do you see yourself?
- Do you give yourself affirmations or are you always beating yourself up and telling yourself how unworthy or ugly or fat etc. you are?

- Again, write down words relating to how you see yourself.

Centre: The centre is about who or what is the focus of your life. It's the identification of what takes up the most time and the thoughts that dominate your day or night.

- Who or what is the focus of your life? Is it your partner, your children, your church, your faith, your work or something else? What should it be?
- Write in the centre who or what is the focus of your life.

Dr Russell stated that it's important that you look after all of these areas. If not, like the chair, you will be unbalanced and something will give.

Before you keep reading, stop and take some time to reflect on your diagram.

- Are you happy with all of your answers?
- Is there something that you need to add or deduct?

And if your answers aren't what you'd wish them to be, consider how you can make changes.

Your social circle

It's not good for humans to be alone. That's why God made Eve for Adam. And yet a recent Relationships Australia study found that one-in-ten Australians currently lack social support. The 2018 Australian Loneliness Report_psychweek.-org.au/loneliness-study/, conducted by the Australian Psychological Society and Swinburne University, found that one-in-four Australians reported feeling lonely each week, one-in-two sometimes or always feel alone and thirty per cent of people say they don't belong to a friendship group.

I think you would agree these statistics show that loneliness is a huge issue in today's society. It proves that you can be surrounded by people but be lonely. You can also have 1,000 or more friends on Facebook or Instagram but still be lonely.

I remember feeling lonely at work. I'd sit at the lunch table and watch the groups around me chatting. None of them invited me into their conversations and, if I tried to join in, I didn't feel welcome. I was surrounded by people but felt like an outsider and lonely and sometimes jealous when they were laughing and having a good time. Once, I was invited into a group due to a joint friendship but, when the friendship dissolved over a disagreement, I was pushed out again. That made sitting at the table even more difficult. At times, I retreated to my classroom.

Research says there's a variety of thoughts on why people feel lonely but, as with most states of the mind, it basically comes down to genetics and one's environment and life experiences.

A genetic vulnerability means that people could have traits which give them a disposition to be lonely such as a poor self-esteem or low mood, anxiety, anger and lower sociability.

Now mix that with the culture we're born into. In cultures where neighbours and societies help each other, people are going to be less likely to feel lonely. People in European social democracies such as Denmark and the Netherlands are said to have greater social integration and their people experience less loneliness. In cultures such as the US and Australia, where the emphasis is on work, mobility, autonomy and individuality, there are higher levels of isolation and loneliness.

Thirdly, people with a history of loss, trauma, inadequate support systems and negative, critical and harsh parenting are also said to experience higher rates of loneliness.

Loneliness occurs due to a lack of connection with other people.

So, how do we broaden our social circle, decrease our susceptibility to loneliness and make genuine friendships?

I've found that the best friendships which are true connections occur where, first, there's a shared interest or something in common and, second, shared values or things that matter most to both people.

For example, you may meet via a craft group or at the school pick up zone or at the local dog park. It might be via a support group for disabilities or even while on the daily commute on the train. Through further conversations and spending time together, you either find you agree with the other person's views and values or you don't. Usually, when a person strongly doesn't like something about the other person, the friendship stops and they stay as acquaintances. But when sharing of life is frequent and each feels heard and supported then the friendship normally flourishes. The friendship may then stay within the setting where it began or it can expand to sharing activities or conversations outside of this.

I was talking to one of my friends at pottery about making friendships. We both agreed that making friends has to be done purposefully. We also discussed the impact of how having low vision can make forming friendships more difficult as it adds another layer of complexity. Maybe you can identify with having added complexity.

Some friendships are found at work but many more are established out in the community, in interest groups, for example, through sport, church, school, Men's shed, hobbies and while volunteering. If we can't go out due to our disability or circumstance, there are online groups.

From personal experience, I know that it can be scary to go somewhere new ... particularly if you're shy or have social anxiety. But, sometimes, the best things in life come from taking calculated risks. This is definitely one of them.

If you need some ideas of where you can find people with similar interests (your 'peeps'), look at these:

- join a club, for example, pottery, darts, gems, photography, bushwalking, Rotary and Lions
- join a gym or exercise group
- join or start a walking group
- join a church activity group
- go to local council activities
- join or start an art or craft group
- join a Men's or Women's Shed
- talk to the other parents at school or join the Parents and Citizens/Friends
- volunteer with a charity
- volunteer at your children's sporting events or school
- while walking your dog, talk to other owners with similar dogs
- study a course or go to workshops on things you are interested in
- join online forums and Facebook groups, Google groups and communities that share your interests

∞∞∞∞

'When you find the people who not only tolerate your quirks but celebrate them with cries of 'Me too!' —be sure to cherish them— because those people are your tribe.' —A.J. Downey, Cutter's Hope

∞∞∞∞

I mentioned above that it can be hard to go somewhere new where you won't know anyone. My acute shyness, social anxiety and dislike of small talk have stopped me in the past from meeting new people. But now, as part of leading my best life, I don't want these things to be barriers, so I've taught myself some strategies. Maybe they will help you too.

Step One: Before I get to the event, I prepare some questions in my mind. For example, if I am going to a writing workshop, an appropriate question would be, 'What type of writing do you do?'

Obviously, if you're going to a club or school etc. then everyone there has a similar interest so questions are easier to come up with. It gets trickier if you're going to a social activity where there isn't a common interest.

The sky's the limit for the questions you can prepare. The only rule, if you call it a rule, is that the questions can't be answered with 'yes' or 'no'. They need to be asked in such a way they elicit a longer response.

To do this, start your questions with Who, What, When, Where, Why or How. After these, you can use, 'Tell me more about…'

If you need some help, here are some ideas which you can form questions about:
- the weather
- their children, if in a school or children's club

- how long they've been going to the club
- if it's a club, their interest or involvement in the activity
- about the church and what they do
- their interests and hobbies
- their work and what they do
- their plans for the weekend

Step Two: Once at the venue, I scan the room as well as I can. If I know someone, I go to them. If I don't then I try to make eye contact with someone and smile. If everyone is in groups or pairs already talking then I take a deep breath and join a group of people who look friendly. Usually, someone will notice me and say hi and we'll make introductions. If I'm completely ignored then I don't take it personally. I move on and try another group or a person on their own. If I approach someone who's on their own then I use one of my prepared questions. I always think that the other person is most likely feeling the same way as me. And I've found that once I've found something that person wants to talk about—and it's normally something about them—I will be fine.

Your physical body

I think most people know that, to look after their physical body, they need to eat nutritional food which is as little processed as possible. It is well documented that eating smaller portion sizes and cutting down on fatty, sugary, salty and high calorie foods will help create and maintain a healthy body.

Nutrition Australia has on its website the recommended dietary guidelines for all ages.

For adults, generally speaking, their daily intake should be:

- 5-6 serves of vegetables and legumes
- 2 serves of fruit
- 4-6 grains (cereals)
- 2-3 lean meat, fish, poultry, eggs, nuts, seeds and beans
- 2.5-4 milk, yoghurt, cheese and alternatives

And, of course, we must remember to drink water. Water is necessary as between 50%-80% of the human body is made up of H_2O. All the body's chemical processes take place in water. We need water for digestion, to absorb nutrients, to help us remove waste products and to regulate our body temperature. If the body doesn't get enough water, dehydration will result—which is problematic. Dehydration can lead to kidney stones, heart valve issues and some kinds of cancer. Even minor dehydration can affect physical and mental performance.

We get about one-fifth of our fluid from food and the rest is drunk. The Australian government recommends adults drink eight to ten cups of fluid a day. You can get water from any fluids—including tea and coffee, fruit juice and soft drinks. Be careful, though, with how much of these other types of fluids you drink as some have added sugar and caffeine which can lead to weight gain, damage your teeth and be stimulants.

If you need extra help in this area, speak to your GP. They can point you in the right direction.

With good nutrition comes exercise. The Australian Government's Department of Health and Aged Care recommends that being active, for adults (18-64 years):

- helps reduce or manage type 2 diabetes and cardiovascular disease

- maintains or improves blood pressure and cholesterol and blood sugar levels
- reduces the risk of some cancers, prevents unhealthy weight gain and helps with weight loss
- maintains strong muscles and bones and creates opportunities for socialising
- helps develop and maintain physical and mental well-being

The department recommends adults should be active most days, preferably every day. Each week, adults should do either:

- 2.5 to 5 hours of moderate intensity physical activity — such as a brisk walk, golf, mowing the lawn or swimming
- 1.25 to 2.5 hours of vigorous intensity physical activity — such as jogging, aerobics, fast cycling, soccer or netball
- an equivalent combination of moderate and vigorous activities including strengthening exercises on at least two days each week such as push ups, pull ups, squats or lunges, lifting weights or household tasks that involve lifting, carrying or digging

Exercise doesn't have to be all about going to the gym or pool. Exercise can be incorporated into your daily activities. For example, walk or ride a bike for short trips, use the stairs instead of the lift, get off one bus stop or one train stop earlier or park further away from the shops so you must walk. Just move your body.

If you are on the NDIS, you may be given funds for exercise physiology and physiotherapy. Or if you are eligible, you can access a Care Plan from your local GP, which provides you with five free sessions to a range of health professionals. The app store also has a number of exercise apps or you can look on YouTube for videos that motivate you.

(Finding time can be an excuse or obstacle so I have included some strategies for organising your priorities and time later in this chapter.)

To maintain your physical body there are also substances and activities that should be eliminated or avoided—smoking, vaping, excessive alcohol use, drugs and gambling. There is plenty of research and public awareness campaigns on how these things destroy lives.

∞∞∞∞

'A calm and undisturbed mind and heart are the life and health of the body.' —Proverbs 14:30

∞∞∞∞

Your mind

The Australian mental health charity, Beyond Blue, reports that 45 percent of people will experience a mental health condition in their lifetime. One-in-four people will be affected by anxiety conditions and one-in-seven will experience depression.

Anxiety and depression, schizophrenia, bipolar mood disorder, personality disorders and eating disorders are all mental illnesses. Each affects the person in its own unique way (there are lists of criteria for how a diagnosis is made) but all have a common element—they significantly affect how a person thinks, feels, behaves and interacts with other people.

Mental illnesses are caused by a combination of factors from things such as life events, how our brain works, genetic factors, birth defects, how we grew up, our environment, social group, culture and our life experiences.

Even though there are a range of mental illnesses, I'm going to just focus on anxiety and depression.

I can tell you matter-of-factly that my anxiety began in childhood. I vividly remember when I was ten years old, post-surgery, and I refused to get out of the car to go into Brownies. I absolutely loved Brownies but I wouldn't go in. I was fearful of what the girls might say about my wig and me. Mum's coaxing was in vain. She recalls how distressed I was and her thankfulness that Brown Owl came to the car, spoke to me, showed me care and love and I went in. I happily continued from that time on.

I'm going to start with explaining what anxiety is and how it's different to being nervous ... and then move on to depression. Please do not use my definitions as a diagnostic tool but, if you identify with what I've written, reach out to a GP or a Mental Health Service for help. There's help available. Mental illnesses are diagnosed through standardised criteria.

Also, don't be embarrassed if you have, or think you may have, anxiety or depression. I know there's a lot of stigma around mental illnesses but think of it this way—if your leg was broken, you'd get it fixed. If you had gallstones, you'd have your gallbladder removed. If you had a headache, you'd take paracetamol. Your brain is just another part of your body and, if it isn't in a good way, go and get help. Get it fixed.

Anxiety. We all know what it's like to feel nervous—when we experience butterflies in our tummy or sweaty palms. We also know that, once we have faced the scary situation, those nervous symptoms go away and may even be replaced by exhilaration or pride in ourselves.

Nerves are normal and everyone experiences them when they step out of their comfort zone or are doing something significant that they don't want to mess up.

Anxiety (or an anxiety disorder) is of a more extreme nature, occurs more frequently and isn't always connected to an obvious challenge the way being nervous is. Because of the intense and frequent nature of symptoms, anxiety impacts a person's quality of life and day-to-day functioning. It can be quite debilitating.

Symptoms include:

- Physical: panic attacks, hot and cold flushes, racing heart, tightening of the chest, quick breathing, restlessness, or feeling tense, wound up and edgy
- Psychological: excessive fear, worry, catastrophizing, or obsessive thinking
- Behavioural: avoidance of situations that make the person feel anxious, which can impact on study, work or their social life

What kinds of anxiety disorders are there? Anxiety disorders are diagnosed by trained professionals such as psychiatrists. My information below is just to bring some awareness so you can get help if you need it and lead your best life.

Here are the four most common types of anxiety disorders. You can have more than one type:

Panic Disorder
Panic attacks are bouts of sudden, intense, overwhelming and often uncontrollable feelings of anxiety. Physical symptoms can include trouble breathing, chest pain, dizziness and sweating. Panic attacks can start in childhood.

Social Anxiety Disorder (Social Phobia)

Social anxiety is more than just shyness or discomfort in social situations. Everyday interactions cause significant anxiety, self-consciousness and embarrassment because the person fears being scrutinised or judged negatively by others. Many people with social anxiety avoid social situations.

Generalised Anxiety Disorder

People with Generalised Anxiety Disorder worry a lot and about lots of different things. As soon as one worry gets resolved, another pops up in its place.

Phobias

A specific phobia is when someone feels very scared about a particular object or situation.

Let's now look at what depression is:

Depression (Clinical depression or Major Depressive Order). We all feel sad sometimes and most likely, at one time or another, we all wish we hadn't been born. This is called a low mood and is different to depression.

The World Health Organisation tells us that, by 2030, depression will be the leading cause of disability globally.

The Black Dog Institute in Australia has reported that suicide is the leading cause of death for Australians aged between 15 and 44 years. That's a sobering thought.

Depression is a mood disorder where the person experiences feelings of sadness and a loss of interest in life which is felt intensely. The feelings go on for **more than two weeks** (so the person feels sad, down and miserable every day). These feelings prevent the person from doing their normal activities and the activities that usually bring them pleasure. A person cannot just 'snap out of' depression.

With the consistent very low mood, there are usually other symptoms such as:
- loss or gain of a lot of weight or a decrease or increase in appetite
- sleep disturbances
- feelings of being slowed down, restless or excessively busy
- feeling tired or having no energy
- feeling worthless or excessively guilty or guilty about things the person should not have been feeling guilty about
- poor concentration or difficulties thinking or being very indecisive
- having recurrent thoughts of suicide or death

Sometimes, people will only have one bout of depression in their lifetime. Others, like me, will have multiple bouts.

If this resonates with you, please, please, *please* go to your GP and talk to them. There is help available. In Australia, there are also websites and helplines you can ring such as:
- Kids Helpline https://kidshelpline.com.au/
- Headspace for teens https://www.headspace.org.au/
- Beyond Blue https://www.beyondblue.org.au/
- Lifeline https://www.lifeline.org.au/
- Black Dog Institute https://www.blackdoginstitute.org.au/

So, how is anxiety and depression managed and treated? For myself, spending time with psychologists has given me the awareness of what's happening and the skills to manage my symptoms. The doctor prescribed an antidepressant which increases the levels of serotonin in my brain and body, helping to regulate my moods and feelings. And I've also had to change my lifestyle—to one with less stress and more 'me time'. I must admit that sometimes it's still a struggle and I battle my brain—but I'm able to better manage things than I did in the past.

Psychologists and Psychiatrists

What do psychologists do?

Before my breakdown in 2013, I would often look at the psychologist business cards at my local doctor's clinic. I wanted to go and see one but I was scared and embarrassed. I knew my head wasn't right. I knew there were things in my past that I needed to deal with. There were things I just couldn't shake on my own. I knew the stress of my life was getting to me. My anxiety and depression was increasing.

But did I make the appointment? No.

I only made the appointment when it was forced upon me by my doctor. He told me that, as part of my recovery, I had to see a psychologist. I had no choice. And I must admit I was relieved I was being made to.

So, why didn't I seek help years before when I knew in my heart I should? It may even have avoided my breakdown.

Because I think there was and still is, to some degree, a stigma around seeking help and being diagnosed with a mental illness. When we look at history, society has viewed people with mental illnesses as being dangerous or abnormal or weak. Prior to our scientific understanding, mental illness was seen as being caused by curses needing religious intervention. Until recently, people were degraded and put in mental asylums away from society. I felt weak admitting my brain was out of control.

Going to a psychologist was life-changing.

I first went for my anxiety and depression but my psychologists have helped me with more than this. The sessions gave me many 'aha' moments. I act this way because of something in my past. I react this way because of something in my past. I have fears because of… I'm a perfectionist because… I married this person because… This is a trigger because… The list goes on. I now understand myself better. And when my anxiety takes over or my past triggers me, I can look at the situation and my reactions and feelings and ask myself, 'Why am I feeling this way?' Therapy does not take my feelings away but I don't go as low as I used to and I know how to manage my mind. (And if I don't feel I can cope, I can ring my psychologist and make an appointment to go and work through it.)

The psychologist cut the invisible heavy chains that held me captive. And each time a chain fell, I felt lighter. It was an amazing experience.

So, what does a psychologist do? To put it simply, they talk to you and you talk to them. There is nothing scary about it. Now, you're probably wondering why would you talk to a stranger about your problems, particularly when you have friends or family you can talk to? Well, psychologists are trained in different types of therapies and questioning techniques which help you to unpack what is at the core of your feelings. You may not realise the reason or the reason may be different to what you think.

In general, going to a psychologist can help a person to:

- change negative thoughts and feelings
- get involved in activities by encouraging them
- develop problem-solving techniques
- speed their recovery
- identify ways to manage their mental and physical well-being

Psychologists can look past the words you're saying. They can pick up on your body language and your tone of voice. They can go deeper. They have the knowledge to explore your issues in a guided way. They're not necessarily going to give you answers but they'll help you to express your needs, your hurts and your wants. And talking to a psychologist is confidential. The psychologist isn't going to gossip about you. You can be as open as you want to. There is no fear of embarrassment. You don't need to keep secrets. You can expose your true self.

If you're in Australia, you can visit your GP and ask for a Mental Health Care Plan. This entitles you to a maximum of ten sessions with a psychologist in a year. These are usually free if you are on a concession card, or at a reduced cost with a Medicare rebate. You can also get five sessions per calendar year with a General Care Plan and some private health funds pay for psychology. It is important to know that a psychologist cannot prescribe medication, only a GP or psychiatrist can.

What do psychiatrists do?

I'll briefly touch on psychiatrists. There may be a time when you, or a loved one, need to see a psychiatrist. This may feel scary because of the stereotype of mad psychiatrists from eras past. I can assure you that seeing a psychiatrist is not scary at all. The ones I've met are friendly and caring. So, to dispel any myths, let's look at what a psychiatrist is and does.

A psychiatrist is a medical doctor who specialises in psychiatry. They diagnose and treat mental illnesses. They evaluate patients to determine whether their symptoms are a result of a physical illness, a combination of physical and mental or just a mental illness. Psychiatrists can prescribe medication and do a variety of therapies to help the patient.

You'll need a referral from your GP to see a psychiatrist and can go as often as you and the psychiatrist feel necessary. In Australia, some psychiatrists bulk bill while others will require you to pay and then you will receive a partial rebate from Medicare. The fees are dependent on the type of appointment.

It was a psychiatrist who diagnosed me as having Generalised Anxiety Disorder and Clinical Depression.

So, what sort of things would you go and see a psychiatrist for? Here are some:

- addictive and substance use disorders
- attention deficit hyperactivity disorder ADHD/ADD
- anxiety disorders
- autism spectrum disorder ASD
- personality disorders (there are ten types grouped into three clusters)
- depression, postpartum depression
- eating disorders
- post-traumatic stress disorder PTSD

Medications

Medications are administered by GPs and psychiatrists and their purpose is to balance the brain.

The brain is the source of anxiety, which manifests as thoughts, but it also affects the brain chemistry in a way that affects future thoughts and the way the entire body operates. When a person has depression, it's believed that the chemical pathways in the brain become imbalanced as a result of the stressors.

Anxiety can be caused by years of experiences and it can also be caused by genetics. Some people's brains, from birth, have trouble creating some of the chemicals that control mood.

Not every person who has anxiety and depression needs medication but, if a person does, they're normally prescribed an antidepressant. This is due to research finding that the anxiety causes specific changes and an imbalance in the chemicals serotonin, norepinephrine and dopamine (these are called neurotransmitters) in the brain. Sedatives, which are only for short-term use, can also be prescribed.

∞∞∞∞

'There are days I drop words of comfort on myself like falling leaves and remember that it is enough to be taken care of by myself.'—Brian Andreas

∞∞∞∞

Your self-care

Put your hand up if you don't do anything for yourself that brings you enjoyment? Ten years ago, my hand would have shot up. But not anymore! I've learnt the hard way that neglect of self equals burnout.

When I think of self-care, the instructions given by flight attendants at the beginning of a flight come to mind. You are told, with a demonstration, that you must put on your oxygen mask first in an emergency and then assist others. In our day-to-day life, self-care activities are our oxygen masks.

Self-care is essentially doing something that you enjoy and brings you happiness. It's about caring for yourself to ensure that your physical and emotional needs are met.

Dr Elizabeth Scott (2020) defined five areas of self-care—physical (your body), social (relationships), mental (stimulates your brain), spiritual (spirituality) and emotional (healthy coping skills). She says that sometimes you might need more self-care in one area than the others.

There are many benefits to self-care. I'm sure most are obvious but research has shown these include avoiding burnout, improving energy levels, reducing or eliminating mental illness and stress, prevention of disease, promoting resilience and helping to maintain your self-confidence and self-esteem.

I cannot stress how much you must be doing self-care activities. How do you take care of your physical and emotional needs?

If you don't do anything for self-care then I strongly urge you to start. Self-care activities don't have to take long, just do them frequently. And, if you're unsure where to start, here's a list of some ideas:

- start a compliments file—document the great things people say about you to read later, or document the good things that happen
- go cloud-watching—lie on your back, relax and watch the sky
- sing

- unplug for an hour—switch everything to airplane mode and free yourself from the constant *bings* of social media and email
- edit your social media feeds and take out any negative people
- take three deep breaths from your abdomen
- dance
- activate your self-soothing system—stroke your own arm or cross your arms over in front of your chest and pat the top of your arms ... or, if that feels too weird, moisturize your arms
- make one small change to your diet for the week—drink an extra glass of water each day or have an extra portion of veggies each meal
- be still—sit somewhere green or near water and be quiet for a few minutes
- get fifteen minutes of sun, especially if you're in a cold climate (use sunscreen if appropriate)
- have a good laugh—read a couple of comic strips that you enjoy
- ride a bike
- do some art or craft
- go for a walk
- take a quick nap
- help someone—carry a bag, open a door or pick up an extra carton of milk for a neighbour
- write out your thoughts for fifteen minutes on anything bothering you
- stroke a pet—if you don't have one, go to the park and find one (but ask first!)

- have a self-date—spend an hour alone doing something that nourishes you (reading, your hobby, visiting a museum or gallery etc)
- ask for help—big or small doesn't matter but reach out
- go out with friends
- have a massage or spa treatment
- take a bath
- do a jigsaw or puzzle
- take yourself to the movies
- read a book
- try journaling
- visualise a more relaxing place—close your eyes and imagine yourself there … what does it look like, feel like?
- go and get your health checks you've been putting off
- do some active relaxation—I was taught the following exercise by my psychologist: Lie on your back and put your hands on your tummy, loosely. Breathe deeply and slowly in for the count of four. Hold your breath for the count of eight. Then slowly let it out to the count of eight, or even longer if you can. This will relax your body after just a few breaths but, just as importantly, it requires your full concentration. This helps relax you because your mind is focused on your breathing, not on your worries or stresses. Do this ten times.
- do box breathing—close your eyes and breathe in through your nose while counting to four (along the top of the box). Hold your breath while slowly counting to four (down the side of the box). Slowly exhale for four (along the bottom of the box). Hold your breath for four seconds (up the side of the box). Repeat the process.

I wish someone had insisted I do self-care activities when I was trying to be supermum of the year — but if they had then I guess I wouldn't be writing this book! Please take this on board. Self-care equals leading your best life.

Your sleep habits

Part of self-care is also getting enough good quality sleep. The one part I hated about having newborns was waking up for the three-hourly feeds and feeling like a walking zombie. I was so happy when they slept through the night! Sleep is so important for our emotional and physical well-being.

Research says that we need between seven to nine hours of sleep a night. This amount allows our body and mind to recharge. Good quality sleep helps the body to remain healthy and staves off diseases. Without enough sleep, the brain cannot function properly — meaning we'll have problems trying to concentrate, think clearly and process memories. We'll also experience more mood swings and delayed reactions. We know, for example, that driving is impaired by tiredness.

Fortunately, there are things we can do to support our sleep habits. Here are some simple strategies from the Sleep Foundation for poor sleepers. Again, this is not medical advice so please go and see a doctor if you're struggling with insomnia or unexplained daytime tiredness:

- use time management strategies so you go to bed earlier
- don't have your technology in the bedroom. Put your phone on charge out in the kitchen so you won't look at it if you wake up in the middle of the night
- have a sleep routine

- have a hot shower
- don't drink excessive alcohol
- limit caffeine before bedtime and, if possible, do not drink after lunch
- exercise four to six hours before bedtime so your body has time to cool down
- use relaxation techniques, prayer or mindfulness activities
- spray lavender on your pillow
- make sure your room is quiet and dark
- carve out at least thirty minutes of wind-down time before bed in which you do something relaxing such as read a book. Dim the lights in the house slightly for an hour or so before bed.
- disconnect from close-range electronic devices such as laptops, phones and tablets because the light from their screens can alert the brain and make it harder to fall asleep
- if you get into bed and cannot fall asleep after twenty minutes, get up and go to another space in the house to do a relaxing activity such as reading or listening to music. Lying in bed awake can create an unhealthy link between your sleeping environment and wakefulness. Instead, you want your bed to conjure sleepy thoughts and feelings only.
- wake up at the same time every day. Even if you have a hard time falling asleep and feel tired in the morning, try to get up at the same time (weekends included). This can help adjust your body's clock and aid in falling asleep at night.
- use your bed only for sleep

If you're having microsleeps or needing to go back to bed for long naps soon after waking up, your GP may refer you to an ENT (Ear, Nose and Throat) or a sleep specialist to have a sleep study done. I did. The results showed I had severe sleep apnea.

If you don't know what sleep apnea is, let me explain. To put it simply, a person with sleep apnea stops breathing or has almost no airflow (apnea) or isn't breathing enough to maintain oxygen levels in the blood (hypopnea). During these events (apneas), the person usually snorts or snores or sounds like someone choking. These apneas cause the person to wake up to breathe (even if they do not remember it) and prevent them from getting into deep sleep. Deep sleep is what we need to be fully rested. Mild apnea is described as having five to fourteen events per hour, moderate apnea is fifteen to twenty-nine and severe apnea is at least thirty events an hour.

There are two different types of sleep apnea. *Obstructive apnea*, which is the most common, is caused by a blockage to the airway—often by the throat muscles relaxing. *Central apnea* is due to the brain not sending proper signals to the muscles that control breathing.

Research has found that one-in five adults have some level of obstructive sleep apnea.

Undiagnosed sleep apnea can cause the following:
- excessive daytime sleepiness (EDS)
- vision problems
- issues with driving
- insomnia
- depression
- heart attack
- stroke
- heart failure and diabetes

Sleep apnea isn't something you can ignore. There are different types of treatments from surgery to medications to the avoidance of alcohol to taking sleeping pills etc—but probably the most common treatment is a CPAP machine, which I use. A CPAP (continuous positive airway pressure) machine keeps the airway open by blowing air into the throat. It isn't the most comfortable thing in the world but using a CPAP machine gave me back my life. I started using one in 2019 and I now have energy, can concentrate and don't need daily naps.

Your boundary setting

I'm a people-pleaser at heart and I want everyone to like me and for them to be happy. But people-pleasing has led me into too often saying, 'Yes, I can' or, 'Yes, you can', even when I didn't want to. People-pleasers often have loose or unhealthy boundaries.

An example of my people-pleasing occurred only recently. I was asked to be the secretary of a club. I instantly said, 'Yes', but, after some reflection on what I was already committed to, I had to backtrack and say, 'No'. When I went back to the person to say I'd changed my mind, the agitated butterflies in my stomach gave me heartburn! The person tried to convince me to change my mind but I stood firm (yay, me!).

Boundary setting is all about putting limits between you and other people. They are personal and people can have rigid, loose, somewhere in between or no boundaries.

Research says we set personal boundaries in seven areas of life and the types of boundaries can be different for each:

- Physical (e.g. who can or can't touch you or who can go through your purse)

- Sexual (e.g. what you sexually do or don't want to do)
- Spiritual (for example, how your beliefs influence what job you'll take or the friends you'll hang out with)
- Relationship (e.g. how you allow others to treat you or what you'll allow them to do around you based on who they are—like a bus driver, husband, mother-in-law, best friend or adult children)
- Legal (e.g. laws you have to follow such as stopping at a red light)
- Emotional (e.g. requests by the boss at work that make you angry because you feel you're already overworked)
- Mental (e.g. handling people who vehemently disagree with your thoughts or beliefs)

If a person has loose or unhealthy boundaries, they will always say 'yes'—but saying yes to everything when you shouldn't can have severe consequences on your mind, body, relationships and finances. To lead your best life, there are times when you must say 'no'. But if you are like me and have trouble saying 'no', how do you say no politely?

A simple strategy I was taught is to use an 'I' statement. For example, 'I value time being at home with my daughter, so I'm *not* going to say yes to volunteering at activities that take me away from her for more than two hours on a weekend.' Using an I statement and saying why is much better than snapping in frustration, 'No, I can't!' I statements give the other person your reasoning and you can speak in a calm voice.

In close relationships with partners, children, family and best friends, it can be hard to say no. We can feel a sense of guilt and selfishness. In these cases, we must remember why we're saying no. Sometimes we can say no but our boundaries are ignored, leading to resentment. This is a tough one to deal with. In these times, I believe we must keep restating our boundary and why we have the boundary.

It can be easy to be wish-washy with boundaries, one time giving in and the next time standing firm, but the aim is always to remain constant. That way, the people involved know what our stance is. And finally, when there's conflict, it's easy to give in. In these circumstances, we need to remember we're not responsible for the other person's reaction. We must tell ourselves, 'I need to set my boundaries for my self-care and that's okay.' Remember, you're aiming to lead your best life.

Let's move on to looking at responses you can give when you're tempted to immediately say 'yes'. Some are:

- 'Thank you for asking me. I can't give you an answer right now. I will get back to you.'
- 'I have to check my calendar.'
- 'Maybe later.'
- 'Who else can help you?'
- 'Have you asked ...?'
- Say yes to part of the request so you are committing to just an element of a request and doing what you know at that time you can do. For example, the church is asking for people to bake for a cake sale and for people to man the stall. You could say, 'I can bake a cake', if you know you can fit that into your current schedule. Later on, if you decide you want to help out with the cake sale on the day, you can tell the organiser.

Your time

Do you have days where everything seems too overwhelming and you feel totally stressed out? There's too many things to get done or they're too big or you don't have the finances or the time… Days when you feel like you haven't had time to breathe.

I remember nights of tossing and turning because worry consumed me. *What if I forgot to do particular tasks or I couldn't accomplish them on time?*

As I have said earlier in this book, I'm a writer of lists. Lists help me greatly because they stop me from fretting about forgetting something important. But having a long list in front of my face can sometimes be overwhelming and add to my stress. Now, I don't want to give up my lists so I've taught myself a strategy—which is similar to Stephen Covey's principle I share with you next. My simple strategy is prioritizing my tasks from most important and urgent down to the ones that can wait until the next day. I write numbers beside each task then work through them systematically.

When I was studying youth work, we were taught about Stephen Covey's principle for prioritising tasks—which I have found is effective. It comes from his book, The Seven Habits of Highly Effective People.

The first step is to draw a table with the four headings, Important & Urgent, Important & Not Urgent, Not Important & Urgent and Not Important & Not Urgent. Next, write your list of tasks on a separate piece of paper (see page 162).

Let's look at the quadrants:

- Quadrant 1 in the top left column is for your important and urgent tasks. These are items that must be dealt with immediately. They have a significant impact on your goals or plans and time pressures. And if you don't deal with them, they will have major consequences for your stress level, and in other areas such as your job security.

- Next to these, Quadrant 2 (top right), is for the important but not urgent items. These are tasks that are important and must be done but don't require your immediate attention as there are no time pressures.
- Below Quadrant 1 in Quadrant 3 (bottom left) are your urgent but unimportant items. These tasks seem to be urgent and important but, when you really think about them, you realise they're not, as they don't contribute to your goals or plans. The aim is to minimize or eliminate these as much as possible.
- In the last quadrant, Quadrant 4 (bottom right), write the unimportant and not urgent tasks. These are the jobs that don't have to be done anytime soon, they usually have little or no value and are basically time-wasters. Your aim is to minimise or eliminate these.

Since my second facial surgery as a young adult, I've hated making phone calls. It's a psychological barrier caused by the poor speech I had after the surgery. People couldn't understand me and I was embarrassed. (People thought my name was Penny or Henny.) Before the surgery, I'd ring everybody and anybody! Even with therapy, it's been a hard one to overcome as 'avoidance is easier' is well entrenched in my psyche. A strategy I've implemented to help myself is doing the hard task first—and usually that hard task is to make a phone call. After I've achieved that task, I can say to myself, 'Look at you go, girl. You did that!', and the rest of the tasks after that seem so much easier. 😊

	Urgent	Not Urgent
Important	Quadrant 1 • Crises • Pressing problems • Firefighting • Major scrap and rework • Deadline-driven projects	Quadrant 2 • Prevention • Production capability activities • Relationship building • Recognising new opportunities • Planning • Recreation
Not Important	Quadrant 3 • Interruptions • Some calls • Some mail • Some reports • Some meetings • Proximate pressing matters • Popular activities • Some scrap & rework	Quadrant 4 • Trivia • Busywork • Some mail • Some phone calls • Time wasters • Pleasant activities

If tasks are large, like renovating a bathroom, things can still seem overwhelming even after prioritising and this can lead to procrastination. So, let's look at a strategy for breaking up large projects or tasks:

- First, break the whole task down into small tasks.
- Second, make lists of what you need to do for each task.

- Third, set timelines and space the workload out over time. If it's a large task, you won't be able to accomplish it all in one day.
- Fourth, let things go to lighten the load or delegate if you can.

A good recent example of this was when I decided my garage needed to be cleaned out so I could use it as my pottery studio. At the same time, my eldest asked if she could move into the spare room which was my film studio. I'd always told her she could move into that room as the girls had shared a bedroom. I couldn't renege because my eldest was six years older and needed her own room. I immediately said, 'That's fine', but it added more work for me. I looked at the garage and the spare room and thought, 'How am I going to achieve this?' The whole task seemed too much for me to do.

I decided that I'd break each room down into mini goals. To begin with, my goal was to empty three boxes or devote an hour to moving and rearranging etc. The next day, I would do the same. On some days, I got enthusiastic and did more. I ticked off my achievements in my diary.

The job took days to complete but was made easier by each smaller part being achieved in stages. I could feel the endorphins kicking in as I saw the progress I was making. At the end, I had my pottery space, my film studio was packed up and moved to the corner of the playroom and my daughter had her own space.

The last thing I'd like to say about prioritising time and tasks is to be flexible. I like to work through my tasks systematically but that's not always possible. There will be phone calls or kids' needs or unexpected interruptions that can affect the amount of planned work or tasks that can be done. Try not to get annoyed or upset by that. Keep calm and reassign them for the next day or when you can.

Your spirituality

Humans have been spiritual since time began. You can see the worshipping and appeasing of gods and general spirituality in all the ancient civilisations.

Today, spirituality is practised in many ways and from a wide variety of religions to yoga and crystals.

As a Christian, my spiritual life centres around my faith in God and what is written in the Bible. I call myself a follower of Jesus and I aim to not get caught up in any of the rituals or politics of religion.

I started my faith journey from birth, being baptised as a baby in the Presbyterian Church. Knowing I was different, I clung to the hope and love that Jesus brought me. Through my schooling years, I attended church, Sunday school and youth group. In university, I attended the campus Christian group and a Presbyterian church. I tried some Pentecostal churches but found them too much for me.

Upon my return to church, when the children were little, my husband and I found support in a friend's Baptist church. We joined in and helped with many activities and I loved the annual women's camp. As adults, we were baptised and professed our faith there. Upon leaving the Baptist Church, our family then attended a Dutch Reformed church for several years.

My philosophy is that Jesus loved everyone, particularly the outcasts of society. He healed the blind, the lame, the lepers and others. He talked to all levels of society and preached love, inclusion and turning from sins. So, as my role model did, I strive to love everyone (though it's not always easy). I also focus on growing and showing the fruits of the spirit which are love, joy, peace, patience, kindness, goodness, faithfulness, gentleness and self-control. I believe that faith is not contained in a building and at the moment am not attending one. Faith is in our heart and is shown by how we treat other people and what we do for others who cannot help themselves.

> My favourite verses in the Bible from Psalm 139"13-16 are:
> *For you create my inmost being*
> *You knit me together in my mother's womb.*
> *I praise you because I am fearfully and wonderfully made;*
> *Your works are wonderful,*
> *I know that full well.*
> *My frame was not hidden from you*
> *When I was made in the secret place*
> *When I was woven together in the depths of the earth.*
> *Your eyes saw my unformed body;*
> *All the days ordained for me were written in your book*
> *Before one of them came to be.*

These are my favourite verses as they tell me that the God who created the universe, the plants, the animals—all living things—knew me and my destiny before I was born. I'm here on Earth because I'm meant to be here. Everything I was, am and will be, are wrapped up in my life purpose. It's these beliefs that have given me the ability to be strong, brave and resilient.

To become more spiritual takes time and commitment. You can be so busy that often it's dinner time and you haven't acknowledged God's existence. I've found that the best thing to do is start and end my day with God. Before you get out of bed, pray for the day and express your thanks at the end of the day. Say grace for each meal. Listen to a devotion on the way to work or before work. Look for signs that God is helping you and acknowledge them. Look after your temple, which is your body. Seek balance in all the ways I discuss in this chapter.

Do a Bible study, attend church or a home group if that suits you. If that doesn't, there are plenty of online sermons, blogs and Bible studies you can listen to, read and do on your own so you can keep learning about God. Stick up affirmations and Bible verses around your house so you remember how good God is and how perfectly imperfect you are. Keep growing in your knowledge of God. Keep seeking God. Keep asking for wisdom and for His will to be done in your life. When you have problems or a decision to make, pray. Also, listen to your gut instinct—that is most likely the Holy Spirit guiding you. And when things are bad and you can't see God in the situation, thank Him that He is in control. I've had to do this many times in my life.

∞∞∞∞

'In all your ways acknowledge Him, and He shall direct your paths.'—Proverbs 3:6

'For God so loved the world that He gave His only begotten Son, that whoever believes in Him should not perish but have everlasting life.'—John 3:16

'God is our refuge and strength, an ever present help in trouble.'
—Psalm 46:1

∞∞∞∞

Your career and family

We all know what this means. It's the old work-life balance thing. This is something I have always struggled with. Do you?

Being a teacher was a 24/7 job. I say this because my brain never turned off and this is true for most teachers. I was always thinking of my students and how I could best teach them. I was buying things at the shops to help in the classroom and, of course, there was the never-ending lesson preparation, marking and report cards.

Even if I wanted to switch off, my brain just went back to my job. I thought going part-time after my youngest was born would help but having a couple of spare days just gave me more time for planning and lesson preparation and thinking about my students! Because my husband wasn't working, my working part-time meant we needed more money so, instead of teaching the two extra days, I ran an eBay store and tutored children. In hindsight, my work-life balance was poor.

The Australian government states that a good work-life balance means you have harmony between the different aspects of your life and the benefits gained from each area are able to support and strengthen the others. The government also reports that many people are learning to blend their work and personal lives successfully. They've called this work-life integration.

I've done some research on how to maintain a good work-life balance. Have a look at these strategies:

- know what's important to you (Is spending long hours at your job your priority or is your family your priority? Do you have time for your hobbies or passions or to meet with friends and family?)
- time management may help (Use calendars, apps and to-do lists. Are there ways you can cut out the time-wasters like culling unnecessary meetings?)
- set boundaries (If you can, don't look at your work emails after work time, turn off your phone and set a time limit for work at home. If need be, learn to say 'no'.)
- if your job is pulling you down and you're on the path to burnout, you may need to switch jobs (Burnout is characterised by emotional exhaustion, a feeling of detachment from work or becoming cynical, reduced efficiency or lacking a sense of achievement. Of course, getting a new job is often easier said than done. I found that getting another job after leaving teaching was difficult. I didn't have experience in any other fields and my low vision and inability to drive prevented me from applying for many of the jobs I was interested in.)
- think about your finances (I talk about them next. Can you go without some things so you don't have to work as much? Can you downsize your house or live further away from the CBD so your rent is less? Can you buy clothes from an op shop? Can you reduce your takeaways or cut out your barista-made coffees? Can you cancel your paid TV subscriptions, get a lower cost phone plan etc?)

- keep up your relationships (Keep spending time with family and friends as much as you can. Ask for their support in dealing with your work issues and stress.)
- look after your mind and body (Aim to eat healthily and exercise.)
- remember to do your self-care activities like read a book, go for a walk in nature or take a nap

Your finances

If only love made the world go round! It might do, in part, but you also need a certain amount of money to live a satisfactory life. When times are tough, you're unemployed, sick, injured, on a pension etc, your finances can cause stress, particularly if you can't pay the never-ending bills. Maybe it's not the amount of pay you receive but you struggle with overspending and impulse buying instead. You may have one credit card, or two, or three ... or use Afterpay on multiple items at once. Society's cashless way of living doesn't help. Once upon a time, the amount of cash in your purse was all you could spend. Not anymore. It's so easy to tap, tap, tap and then realise you haven't got enough money left for the bills, the rent or mortgage and essentials.

Keeping a reign on your finances takes self-restraint and it's important to know where you're spending your money.

It's always good to spend less than the amount you earn but that can be difficult when you're on a limited income.

I put my hand up to being a reformed impulse buyer. To stop impulse buying and temptation, I don't go to the shops unless I need something. When grocery shopping, I have a list and I look for the specials. For online shopping, I research to find the cheapest price. And I go op shopping.

A Budget. Everyone should have a budget but many of us don't. Some churches offer budgeting advice. In Australia, you can get help from a free financial counsellor by contacting the National Debt Helpline on 1800 007 007 or learn more from their website at https://ndh.org.au/. There are lots of companies who'll help in the creation of a budget but they charge for their services.

But budgets are pretty basic. You don't need to spend money going to a company to have one created. You can do it yourself. I think the hardest part is probably having the self-discipline to sit down and fill one in, and being honest to yourself about your spending habits. Below and on the next two pages you will find a simple budgeting template that you can use to get started. If you don't already have a budget, go ahead and give it a go.

When you have finished filling in your budget, look at it carefully:

- If the money you receive is greater than your expenses, that's great and you can put the excess amount away in savings or for paying for other things you need. You're doing well.

Money I Receive Fortnightly

Pension/Benefit	$
Family/Parenting Allowance	$
Child Support	$
Wages	$
Other	$
Total Fortnightly Income	$

Money I Spend Fortnightly

Roof Over My Head		*Health and Medical*		*Personal Spending*	
Rent/Mortgage	$	Doctor	$	Cigarettes	$
Electricity	$	Chemist	$	Alcohol	$
Gas	$			Magazines	$
Phone	$			Savings	$
Mobile	$				
Insurance	$				
Total	$	Total	$	Total	$
Food		*Clothing*		*Other Purchases*	
Groceries	$	Parent 1	$		$
Corner Store	$	Parent 2	$		$
Meat	$	Children	$		$
Fruit/veggies	$				
Total	$	Total	$	Total	$
Transport		*Entertainment*		*Other Payments*	
Fares	$	Outings	$	Bond Loan	$
Car Payment	$	Takeaways	$	Personal Loan	$
Rego	$			Friends Loan	$
Petrol	$			Credit Cards	$
Repairs	$				
Insurance	$				
Total	$	Total	$	Total	$

Total Expenses

A roof over my head	$
Health/medical	$
Personal spending	$
Food/groceries	$
Clothing	$
Other purchases	$
Transport	$

Entertainment	$
Other payments	$
Kids	$
Birthdays/gifts	$
Total Spent	$

Is there Money Left Over?

Total of money I receive	$
Total of money I spend	$
GRAND TOTAL	$

- If the money you spend is greater than what you earn or receive from the government, then you don't have enough money to live on. This is obviously a problem. When you don't have enough money to live on, you will either need to earn more money, cut back on items in the budget and/or seek professional help like seeing the bank about payments on your mortgage.

Financial Help. If you're having financial difficulty with paying for your expenses such as phone, electricity, rates, water and mortgage, don't just ignore these bills as they won't go away. Ring the company or bank and tell them. By law, they must help you. If you're not in Australia but living in another country, ask around to find out what options are available to you.

If you're on a low income and something happens like your washing machine dies and you need a new one, instead of getting a payday loan (which are high interest loans), a personal loan or using your credit card, in Australia you can apply for a NILS (nil interest) loan from various organisations. See this website for more details: http://nils.com.au/

Have Multiple Bank Accounts. Another strategy, as part two to your budget, could be to make multiple bank accounts which have nicknames. You could have one account for bills, one for a holiday, one for entertainment, one for food etc. Or, if you like withdrawing cash from the bank, you could use glass bottles or envelopes where the money is split into different categories.

∞∞∞∞

In this chapter, we've looked at ways to keep balanced—to always have the four legs of our chair on the floor. We examined our social circles, physical and mental health, the importance of self-care, how to set boundaries and to prioritise our time, spirituality, maintaining a work-life balance and how to budget. There are so many strategies to help us lead our best life!

In Chapter 6, we're going to look at how to be weirdly wonderfully resilient.

Chapter 6 - Be *Weirdly Wonderfully Resilient*

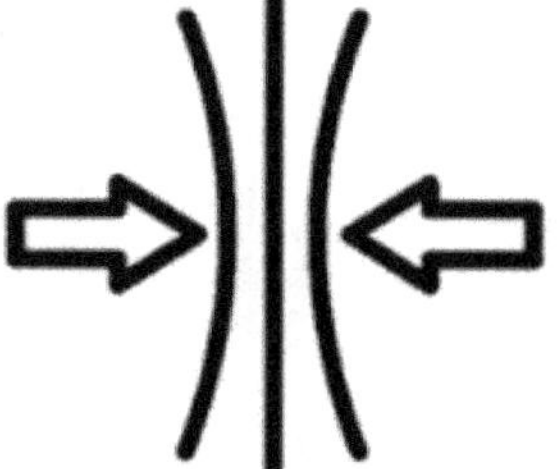

'The difference between a strong man and a weak one is that the former does not give up after a defeat.'—Woodrow

'The righteous keep moving forward, and those with clean hands become stronger and stronger.'—Job 17:9

∞∞∞∞

Have you ever had something horrible happen and you don't know how you're going to recover from it or move forward?

Were you able to bounce back from the situation or even bounce forward?

I have found that when I'm in the midst of pain, trauma, crisis or in the depths of depression, it can be really difficult to see a way forward. In fact, it's often much easier to wallow and feel like giving up.

Research has shown that people who can keep moving forward:

- are better able to heal
- stay mentally and physically healthy
- maintain mobility and cognitive function

These people are being resilient.

The word 'resilience' actually comes from the Latin word resilire ('recoil'). To resile literally means to bounce back, rebound or resume shape after compression. If you think of a soft rubber ball being pushed in, it will spring back out to its round form. It is resilient. If it wasn't resilient, it would stay compressed or pushed in.

I clearly remember flying to Sydney on my own with my white cane, which I have previously mentioned. I'd never been solo anywhere further than a couple of hours away from home. I was anxious but my goal was to attend a bootcamp to gain more skills as a professional speaker. I knew the task involved much more than just flying there.

With pre-organisation and on-the-ground assistance, all went well with the flight and getting to my accommodation.

I was pumped! 'Go girl. You can do this,' I said to myself as I surveyed my apartment. It was under a set of stairs with no window out—just a single bed, bathroom and small kitchenette—all that I needed.

My next task was to find the grocery store. That was more of a struggle as I was new to using my phone's GPS but, after asking people for directions, I found the Metro. 'Yay!'

I spent a fair amount of time searching for some gluten-free dinners (I am Coeliac) and I forgot to keep an eye on the time… This normally wouldn't have been a problem but I was on a time schedule. I'd booked a walking tour of The Rocks for that afternoon. As a middle-school primary school teacher, I'd spent many years teaching students about old Sydney town and the first European settlement in Australia.

'I'm actually going to walk on 1800s cobblestone streets and see the colonial houses and stores!' I told my friends before I left.

I was beyond excited.

I gasped when I read the time on my watch. I'd taken way too long in the grocery store! I had forty-five minutes to return my groceries to my hotel room and reach the meeting spot which was out of the CBD. My heart became like a bucking bronco in my chest. Oh, my goodness! I couldn't miss the tour!

I power-walked back to my room, packed my groceries away, locked the door and scurried to the lift. As I pressed the button to go down, I realised I'd left my cane in my room so I retraced my steps, retrieved it and hurried back to the lift.

Once outside the hotel and standing on the footpath with people bustling past me, I typed the address into the GPS and took off power-walking! I swung my cane back and forth, back and forth. I felt good. It was going to be tight but I was going to make it.

That was until two blocks on. The sun was obscuring the screen and I couldn't hear the audio. I stepped into the shade and tried to decipher the map…

The bucking broncos suddenly became mad bucking bulls on an insane amount of steroids. I couldn't figure out where to go! My watch told me that I had twenty minutes left and I was still in the CBD, confused and freaking out!

My head began to spin as a panic attack threatened. I brought my phone up to my face, trying to see the path—but it was nearly impossible. I told myself to calm down…

And then, of all things … my phone lost its signal!

I swore and my fingers trembled as I reprogrammed the GPS.

The minutes ticked by.

I sighed as I was back on track and began power-walking again.

Now, I have a pretty good sense of direction and, after a couple of streets, wondered why I was walking back towards the CBD instead of out to The Rocks.

'This can't be the way!' I muttered. Tears welled in my eyes. My bucket list walking tour was fading like the sunset.

I scooted along the road looking for a street sign but couldn't find one in the vicinity.

By this time, panic had engulfed me.

I couldn't think clearly and my phone dropped its signal again.

In despair, I retyped our meeting point and it wanted me to backtrack again towards the centre of the city. I knew that wasn't where The Rocks was.

Ten minutes!

Tears dripped down my cheeks.

What was I going to do?

I decided to scrap the GPS and ask a well-dressed lady who stood at the lights waiting to cross the road. She looked at my cane then kindly searched for The Bell Tower in The Rocks on her phone and told me how to get there (apparently there is more than one bell tower in Sydney…)

I took in her directions and, for the first time ever, ran with my cane swinging out from side to side in front of me. People stared at me. I must have made quite a sight but I didn't care. My cane even flew up in the air and hit a lady on the back of her head, which embarrassed me immensely, but I pretended not to notice as I scooted by.

Three-fifteen.

I arrived at the meeting point, gasping for air. No one was there. I was fifteen minutes late. Would I still be able to join?

'Am I too late?' burst from my mouth as I pushed open the tour guide door.

'You're Jenny?'

I nodded.

'They've just left. You'll find them in the lane across the zebra crossing.'

Breathless, I thanked the receptionist and scurried out of the building, across the zebra crossing and turned left into the lane. Ahead of me, a gentleman with a clipboard was talking to a young guy.

'Excuse me, are you The Rocks tour?' I asked them.

'Yes,' they replied. 'You're Jenny?'

'Yes,' I replied. I smiled.

I can laugh at this event now but it was so traumatic at the time and I'll never forget it—particularly my horror of accidentally hitting the lady in the head with my cane.

There are several ways I could have gone on after this experience. I could choose to not go anywhere without a support person. I could choose to not go anywhere new on my own. I could choose to never use a GPS again. I could choose to use the experience to learn a life lesson.

What do you think I did?

Yes, I chose to learn a lesson from my experience. Later that day, after I'd calmed down, I reflected on the experience and thought about what happened to me and why. I hadn't allowed myself enough time, I hadn't looked on a map beforehand to know where I was going in case the GPS was wrong, I couldn't read the screen and the signal dropped out. And I hadn't practised enough with the GPS to fully understand it.

From these lessons, I decided that the next time I travelled alone I would:

- set an alarm when I'm on a limited timeframe
- catch a taxi or Uber if I'm short of time
- spend more time practising using the GPS
- contact Guide Dogs about getting more orientation and mobility training.

Apart from learning lessons from this situation, I also became much more confident. Did you know diamonds are formed under immense pressure? Even though things went wrong, I overcame them. This experience showed me that I could overcome challenges on my own. How freeing, that was!

According to the research of leading psychologist Susan Kobasa, there are three elements that are essential to resilience:

- **Challenge.** Resilient people view a difficulty as a challenge, not as a paralysing event. They see them as lessons to be learnt from, and as opportunities for growth, just as I did in Sydney. They never view difficulty as a negative reflection on their abilities or self-worth.

- **Commitment**. Resilient people are committed to all aspects of their lives. This means they're committed to their relationships, their work, their finances, spirituality, health etc. They're also committed to their goals. Commitment can be hard when setbacks and knockbacks occur but being resilient means they keep going forward.
- **Personal Control**. Resilient people focus on situations and events they have control over. They don't worry over things they can't change such as the weather. This can be hard but it's necessary.

An example of this was when my eldest daughter underwent eye muscle surgery a few years ago and, upon discharge, was told she'd have a number of medications to take home. The medications were delivered to the ward and she was discharged.

Upon reaching home, which was an hour-and-a-half away, I sat down to have a cup of coffee and relax. Maeve found me and said, 'Mum, you need to go back to the hospital. They didn't give me all my meds.'

I set my cup of coffee down and picked my chin up off the floor. As you could imagine, I was a wee bit annoyed as this shouldn't have happened and it would mean over three hours of travel on public transport… But my daughter needed the meds so I chugged the rest of my drink and power-walked to the train station so I could catch the next train.

At the ward, I politely told the nurses about the inconvenience this had caused me but I understood these things can happen. I've been taking my children to the hospital for over twenty years so I know they certainly can! I could have become angry and yelled at the nurses or lodged a complaint but I saw it for what it was and let it go.

I want you to think of a time when you were resilient. If you're saying to yourself, 'I'm not resilient', then think more deeply. You're alive so you must have been resilient at some stage.

Once you have thought of an occasion, reflect on what happened and ask yourself the following questions:

- How did you manage to be resilient?
- Who helped you see your resilience and strengths?
- In what ways are you a different person because of that experience?
- How did your relationships with others consequently change?
- What important lessons about life did you learn?

Personally reflecting on experiences can give you an insight into who you are and your strengths. Reflecting can also provide you with the strength to be resilient in the future. 'I did it last time and I can do it again.'

Resilience has been the subject of hundreds of studies, all with similar findings—that resilient people have social supports, make meaning from the event, manage their emotions and have effective coping strategies. Let's now look at these findings in more detail.

Make meaning from an event

Lots of bad stuff can happen to us. Some things we cause ourselves, some things are caused by people we know and other things are caused by strangers or natural events.

Resilient people learn from their mistakes and failings. (I talked more about learning from mistakes as they don't define you in Chapter 2.) Resilient people also look at what they've been through and construct a life lesson from it or see a purpose for why it's happening. And people who are finding meaning in what's happening keep everything in perspective.

You can see this strategy at work in how I reflected on my Sydney experience. I didn't get angry or make a mountain out of a mole hill. I learnt from it and kept the event in perspective.

Now, don't get me wrong, I'm a realist here. A cancer diagnosis or a loved-one passing away unexpectedly or financial hardships can sometimes seem impossible to find any meaning from. I get it. I've been there. But the research says that, if you can make meaning from the event, not remain bitter or angry but keep moving forward then you are going to be in a much better place mentally and emotionally than if you don't. Something to think about.

∞∞∞∞

'Accept, then act. Whatever the present moment contains, embrace it as if you had chosen it. This will miraculously change your whole life.'—Eckhart Tolle

∞∞∞∞

Cope with change

I don't know if anyone really likes change. Change is usually not easy as it often means moving out of your comfort zone; it means doing things differently from how things are normally done and it can evoke a wide range of emotions.

Of course, there is a spectrum in 'change' from slight to significant and where the situation sits on this spectrum will determine how easy it is cope with. But no matter where the event sits on the spectrum, you must come to terms with the change, deal with it and keep moving forward. Resilience and leading your best life, go hand in hand with embracing change.

My youngest is a creature of routine. Jessica gets up at the same time, she eats morning tea, lunch and afternoon tea at the same time. She eats the same things each day for meals except dinner. She has a particular sequence of events before she goes to bed. It's the same in the morning before she goes to school and on weekends… And, due to the rigidity of her routine caused by her autism, breaking or changing it used to cause a lot of angst for her and for me. For example, she couldn't understand why she might have to eat dinner earlier because of going to swim club. This would cause a meltdown. There were times she didn't want to go somewhere because she was going to miss morning tea which is at 10:00 a.m. sharp.

Though we didn't see it that way at the time, a hidden blessing of COVID-19 for us came when specific food items that my daughter loved were completely out of stock — chicken nuggets and hash browns. I searched all grocery stores within our area for these elusive golden-ticket items but to no avail. Jessica became upset but had no choice but to go with the change of foods. She complained. She hated it but, in the end, she accepted it.

This then opened the door to widening her food choices, which became more freeing for her and us.

In addition, she participated in swimming at the Special Olympics National Games in Tasmania in 2022. I was concerned about how she would cope with all the changes and particularly the food. I decided I wouldn't pack extra food for her. She had to eat what was provided. How do you think she went?

During the event, her support worker smiled and told me, 'She's eating everything!'

And Jessica, with a big grin on her face, exclaimed, 'I made toast with vegemite for breakfast!'

I was ecstatic! I believe the changes that occurred during the pandemic showed her that she could eat different foods and be okay. She also coped well with the constant changes to her daily routine during the week she was away. It led to a good experience for her in the pool with Jessica winning a national gold medal and two silvers. Her mindset during the games told her 'change was okay' and she embraced it.

Change is scary but change is growth.

If you also have trouble coping with change, here are some strategies which I believe will help you:
- acknowledge that things are changing
- prepare yourself (Create your lists, save money if your situation is finance related and talk to people who can help you. Also, instigate your problem-solving and making good choices strategies which I've talked about earlier in the book.)
- change how you're thinking about the situation (If you immediately slump into negative thinking and a woe-is-me attitude then coping with the change is going to be more difficult. If you engage your positive thinking and look for the good or the advantages in the situation then you're going to cope with the change much more easily.)

- gather a support network around you (This is particularly important if the change is related to your health.)
- keep up your healthy eating, exercise and self-care activities

Be a problem-solver

Being resilient often incorporates having to problem-solve to find the best way forward. Problem-solving is similar to making decisions, which I talked about in Chapter 3, and both skills are needed for you to lead your best life.

While researching, I've found seven steps that are most commonly involved in problem-solving. They are:

1. State the problem.
2. Identify what needs to be solved. If the problem is large, break it down into smaller parts.
3. Think of as many possible solutions as you can. This is called brainstorming. Write them down.
4. Evaluate each possible solution by identifying their pros and cons.
5. Select the best option. There may need to be multiple solutions or steps.
6. Implement the solution or steps. This will most likely involve planning and then execution.
7. Look at the results or outcomes and evaluate whether the problem-solving steps worked or not. If they didn't, you may need to go back to your list and try again or ask someone for help.

Problems only get solved when you stop ignoring them.

You can see in these steps there are similarities between problem-solving and making good decisions.

I've found that brainstorming (Step 3) is important to implement as it provides time before taking action. It prevents us from using the first solution that pops into our head, which could be made based on emotions, fear or irrationality. Brainstorming, as a strategy, allows freedom for the brain to be creative. In this step, it doesn't matter how silly a solution sounds, it still gets written down.

When deciding on the solution, flexibility is key. You don't want to be rigid or unwilling to step out of your comfort zone. Be open-minded.

Where disability and difference are involved, the term 'dignity of risk' is sometimes used.

Dignity of risk refers to the legal right of every person, including those with disability, to make choices and take risks in order to learn, grow and have a better quality of life.

With people requiring support, dignity of risk and duty of care go together. Basically, if the choice doesn't put the person with disability at risk of serious injury or death, the person needs to be able to action their choice. If, after actioning their choice, there are consequences then, like neurotypical people, the person would need to deal with these. I call dignity of risk the, 'don't wrap disabled people up in cottonwool theory'.

When being a problem-solver, the overarching principle is to *keep your mindset positive*. If you want to read more about positive thinking, go back to Chapter 2. Being positive, though not always easy, will allow your mind to come up with solutions and help move you forward. It will enable you to be resilient.

A positive attitude is the only option if we want to problem-solve.

Take risks

Last year, my partner, Ken, and I went bushwalking in the beautiful scenic rim behind the Gold Coast. There was a light sprinkling of rain but that wasn't going to dampen our excitement of exploring the nature trails. We had our trusty travel brochure, drink bottles and an umbrella.

We arrived at the first trail, met by a grassy parking area at the end of a road with no visible signs to indicate it was a bushwalk.

'This is awesome!' I said. 'It's not one that everybody does.'

According to the map, our reward at the end of the walk was a magnificent waterfall.

I shoved my water bottle in my front pocket and held my white cane in my right hand.

The walk was beautiful. Ken stopped to show me fungi and other things he thought I'd be interested in.

High stairs were scaled and rocks climbed over. I used my cane for balance and as a walking pole and was pumped that, even with my low vision, I was still able to be adventurous. I hadn't done anything like this in over twenty years.

We arrived at the waterfall and, as a result of the recent rain, it was breathtakingly amazing. We drank from the crystal clear cool flowing water and lapped up the ambience of the forest. Heaven on Earth.

Spits of rain, which became heavier, saw us cuddling against a tree under our umbrella until it subsided. Though thoroughly romantic with the gorgeous smell of the forest filling my nostrils and the burbling of the creek, time was ticking on. We'd planned to walk another trail after this one so we headed back.

With the downpour, the dirt trail had become muddy and slippery. I kept using my white cane as a walking pole and followed Ken's shoes so I wouldn't trip or fall over a tree root or rock. I didn't look up and around unless he stopped to show me something. He was very good at telling me there were obstacles and helping me when needed.

At one point, Ken told me sharply, 'Stay to the right. Do not take a step to the left.'

I stopped, wondering what was going on, turned my head to the left and freaked out! If I'd taken one small step to the left, my blind side, I'd have slipped down the mountain. I gasped as the realisation of the danger, which I was unaware of, hit me.

With adrenaline pumping through my veins like white-water rapids, I made it back to the car and we continued on. Back in the hotel, we reread the trail map information and saw the bushwalk was classed as a Category 4, which explained the terrain. I gulped then grinned, shaken by the danger and super proud of myself for accomplishing the challenge.

A risk is a situation involving exposure to danger.

Every day, we take risks. When we cross the road, when we charge our e-scooter, when we give out our credit card details on the Internet, when we eat leftovers from the fridge, when we swim at the beach etc.

Most of the risks we take are done without thinking, like driving a car, but some are calculated and planned for. For example, we swim between the lifesaving flags at the beach because we know there's a risk of rips and drowning. If we get into trouble between the flags, the lifesavers will come to rescue us.

Resilience is built when a person can manage their risks and bounce back from failed ones.

Risks are everywhere and cannot be avoided. The Earth and society are unpredictable in many ways. Earth floods, has hurricanes, deep freezes, droughts and fires. The economy and world markets fluctuate. Employment is not 100% guaranteed, nor is good health.

Being able to assess risks without having to use too much thought helps us with our day-to-day activities. For example, it's a heatwave so I decide to skip my lunchtime run. I use my instincts and my learnt skills to manage the risk of heatstroke.

Being able to assess risks with more thought helps us with our more complex and long-term risks like buying a house, starting a business or investing in shares. The risks involved in making these decisions will have financial, emotional and psychological consequences.

Positives of calculated risk-taking. Some people, including myself, have looked at the consequences of a risk and decided the consequences are too scary to contemplate so they've snuggled deep into their comfort zone and not taken any. This is fine if they're happy but what if you aren't? Let's look at an example. Say I'm unhappy in my job but I'm fearful of being unemployed. What do I do? I stay there, feeling miserable.

What if, on the other hand, I decided to take a calculated risk and take leave so I can look for another job?

A calculated risk, as explained by the Merriam-Webster dictionary, is *a hazard or chance of failure whose degree of probability has been reckoned or estimated before some undertaking is entered upon.*

In regards to leaving my job, my calculated risk would be based on research. First, I would look into my leave. I find out that I have three months which I am allowed to take. Second, I look at my finances and my savings. I calculate that I have enough to last me six months of unemployment. So, after careful consideration, I decide that I will take leave and look for another job. If I don't find something else, at least I've had a break which I needed.

Research has shown many benefits of taking calculated risks. These include an increase in our self-confidence, the ability to learn new skills—because we move out of our comfort zone—and financial reward if it is investment related. Can you think of others?

I must add here a cautionary note... It's important to remember, when taking risks, that success won't come every time. Sometimes risk-taking has negative consequences and leads to failure—there are no guarantees. Read on...

Learn from negative experiences and failure

Being resilient requires you to deal with, and move forward past, negative experiences. Ignoring they ever happened does not promote resilience.

I can tell you from my own experience that, if you push your negative experiences down and pretend they never happened, you'll explode like an erupting volcano as soon as you're triggered—which could happen anywhere at any time.

Instead of ignoring a negative experience, one trick is to look at the situation as if you're someone else. In third person or 'God status', so to speak, then ask yourself:

- What went wrong?
- What is really at stake?

- What can you learn from this to do differently next time?

Asking these questions from an outsider's perspective, helps us to remain calm and rational, and to have a logical and honest mind.

In my opinion, using the negative experience as a learning tool is the best way to go.

Failure is not the opposite of success. It is part of success.

I still remember the very first time I flunked an exam in high school. It was a biology test in Year 10. It hit me hard. Since then, there have been more times in my life when I've tried and been unsuccessful or failed — whether it was a lesson I was teaching that didn't achieve its desired outcome, a student I thought I could help but wasn't able to, trying to throw a pot on the wheel (so many failures!), planting strawberries which quickly died, having short stories rejected by publishers or not getting the job I was told was mine. Oh, boy, I could write a book about my failures and maybe you could, too!

∞∞∞∞

'We learn wisdom from failure much more than from success. We often discover what will do by finding out what will not do; and probably he who never made a mistake never made a discovery.' — Samuel Smiles

∞∞∞∞

Numerous resilience-building strategies are available from research, to help you recover from failures. Many of these I have touched on already. They are:

- **Be open.** Even though most people hate failure, it's absolutely okay to fail. Failure can actually be good. Why? Because it can give you valuable lessons from the process. Sometimes you learn what you need to do and other times you may learn what not to do again. Ultimately, failure brings personal growth and new understandings.

- A while ago I was watching the morning TV and Boy George was being interviewed about being on The Voice, a singing talent show. He said, 'Failure is education', and I totally agree with him. (I knew it wasn't just Boy George 'being different' that drew me to him as a teenager!) You can gain wisdom and grow in resilience. It can lead you to change directions in life and this change will quite possibly lead you to a better place.

- As a Christian, I believe God has you under His care and is directing your path. He knows that you're going to fail and will often use this to take you where you need to go to fulfil your life purpose.

- **Welcome failure.** That might sound absurd but research says that failure allows you to experience the self-satisfaction and joy of succeeding. If you didn't fail, you wouldn't understand and have the euphoria of success!

- **Failure helps you to make priorities in life**. When you fail, as a teenager or an adult, you start to question what you really want in life and if the dreams you have for your future are achievable. You may decide you need to work harder or maybe you need to change directions and try something new. Failure forces you to look at yourself and think about or identify the things that really matter to you and the things that you value.

- **If the failure is caused by a shut door, rephrase the 'No'.** What I mean by this is if you have your heart set on doing something and you get told, 'No,' try to rephrase the negative into a positive. How about 'no' meaning 'next opportunity'? Look for what is coming next.

- **Many others throughout history have failed and many didn't give up.** In fact, many people who experienced failure and kept going went on to achieve great things. For example, Henry Ford's first two companies failed. The first one went bankrupt and the second one ended after a big dispute. Ford walked away from that company with only the rights to his name. But it was his third try that really sealed the deal. He was so passionate about his mission that he refused to give up. Bill Gates suffered failure in his first business but this didn't discourage him from trying again. He didn't give up because the sheer notion of business intrigued him. The next company, which we all know, was Microsoft.

∞∞∞∞

'The master has failed more times than the beginner has ever tried.'—Stephen McCranie

'Every failure is a step to success.' —William Whewell

∞∞∞∞

- **You're able to look at obstacles differently.** Passion drove both Ford and Gates. They also believed in themselves and their abilities and, at each setback, grew more determined to see their dreams come to fruition. They were resilient. This is something for you to think about.

A quick story of my own here. I had a tough first year of teaching. It was a shock coming to the suburbs from a large country town. I'd never had to deal with challenging children. I struggled with shyness, social anxiety, lack of self-confidence and first-year nerves. I worked cooperatively with a colleague but that didn't work out. I also didn't feel supported by the principal who I felt didn't like me and made my life difficult.

I believed I was a hardworking, good teacher. I wasn't perfect, had a lot to learn and was trying my best at gaining as many on-the-job skills as I could. The other teachers believed I was doing well and my students' parents liked me.

One day, the principal told me, 'I'm going to fail you so you should resign and get a different job.'

What?!? Horror, fear and anger coursed through me. I didn't want to do something else. I'd wanted to be a teacher ever since my childhood and I loved the profession.

That principal left soon after this conversation and another one transferred in. The new principal showed me a different attitude. She took me under her wing and believed in me as I believed in myself. The first principal had battered my ego and self-confidence and the second principal, knowing this, gave me lots of affirmations and practical guidance.

I passed my probationary period the following year. I then went on to teach and nurture hundreds of children over twenty-five years of service.

My message is: don't give up just because someone discourages you. Try your hardest to make things work.

Sometimes, though, even after trying hard, things don't work out … but that's okay because you're resilient.

Have effective coping strategies

Everyone needs an arsenal of coping strategies to be resilient. What are yours?

Do you go shopping, stress eat, bite your nails, go for a walk, do yoga or take a drive in the country?

If you have a coping strategy, is it working for you? I'm a nail biter and a stress eater. I have to say that those strategies give me immediate relief but, afterwards, I'm annoyed with myself and wish I hadn't done either.

If your strategies are unhelpful then maybe it's time to think of some other things you can do.

For example:

- going for a walk
- doing a relaxation exercise
- gardening
- having a fidget or squeeze toy in your bag
- exercising
- doing a creative activity

There are more ideas for you in Chapter 5 under self-care and in Chapter 4 under mindfulness.

Obviously, your strategy will depend on where you are when your negative emotions hit. You may need different strategies for different situations or places.

When I'm out-and-about, one of my coping strategies for the beginning of a panic attack is to stop and look around me. I focus on something external, like naming three things that I can see, feel, hear, touch or smell, and take some deep breaths. I then try to think calmly and problem-solve the situation.

When I'm feeling overwhelmed at home, one of my coping strategies is to leave the house. Just going for a walk, to an op shop or to the beach always helps break my anxiety, the loop in my brain or low mood.

I must admit there are times when the above strategies just don't work—usually when triggers are traumatising me and, no matter what I try, I can't stop them. For these events, I use the strategy below called the book and bookshelf metaphor. This was taught to me by a psychologist.

Book and Bookshelf metaphor. First of all, imagine your life as a book or a series of books. As a book, each chapter is a time period or major event in your life. As a series of books, each book would be a time period.

I chose to use a series of books as I can clearly divide my life up into distinct stages—birth to 18 years, 1986/university to 1999/end of my first marriage, 1999/my second marriage to 2021/death of my husband, 2021 to the present.

Now, imagine this book or your books are sitting on a bookshelf. They look all shiny and bright, maybe even with gold-embossed spines. My books have rainbows and sparkles on them.

When an event in your history is triggered, the book with that event pops itself off the bookshelf and opens to the corresponding chapter and you are reminded of what happened. I get visuals as if I was back there at that time. This can be very confronting, particularly if it was a traumatic or negative experience.

So, why does this happen?

As it was explained to me, this remembrance of the situation is your brain's way of trying to protect you from making the same mistake again or having that traumatic event reoccur. That's why your brain shows you the event. For example, your brain could be saying, 'Remember last time you dived off the blocks—you did a huge belly-flop, your tummy smacked the water and you experienced a great amount of pain.' You don't want to do a belly-flop again so you don't dive. This is a simple example but it relates to Jessica who developed a fear of diving due to repeated belly-flops.

A personal example of this occurred two years ago when I began karate. In the first lesson, I was majorly triggered while watching Sensei demonstrate the basic punches and blocks. While he innocently clenched his hands to show us the punching technique, my brain shot me straight back to the 1980s and into the middle of my first coercive control marriage. In this marriage, my husband and I were both into karate … but he would use the karate at home to intimidate and control me. For example, he would throw punches at my face and pull back just before they connected. My brain superimposed my husband onto Sensei. A panic attack instantly enveloped me. My heart hammered, my palms sweated and I couldn't concentrate. I wanted to run and never return.

During the week, I was able to speak to my psychologist about this experience. She explained what was happening and gave me the book metaphor.

'Okay,' I said, 'so, how do I deal with this?'

'You need to acknowledge it's your brain trying to protect you, and speak to your brain.'

She gave me an example. *Thank you brain for the reminder. I know you're trying to protect me but I learnt my lesson from that situation. It's that I'll never be in a relationship where I'm not treated respectfully and I'm not going to repeat it.*

'Then you tell your brain why you're in the current situation.'

I'm learning karate so I can be healthy and feel more confident when I am out and above. I'm moving forward on to my strong, resilient, happy, independent self.

The psychologist emphasised to me that the last step is very important and shouldn't be missed. We must remind our brain that we're moving forward—we're not staying in the past.

It's helpful to visualise the book being placed back on the bookshelf.

The next week, I went back to karate with a positive mindset. During the lesson, I experienced more triggers. I visualised putting the book back on the bookshelf and told my brain why I was doing karate … but, to my horror, the book kept popping off the bookshelf! It wouldn't stay there. This greatly distressed me and I spoke to my psychologist again.

Her advice in this instance, was to tell my brain: *Okay brain, I am moving forward on to being my … independent, strong self. If you don't want to pop this memory away in the bookshelf then the book can stay out and open. But I'm not going to focus on the book. I'm going to focus on what I'm doing. I'm … learning karate to get fit, gain confidence and to be able to defend myself.*

Visualising laying the book aside eased my distress and I could continue karate. My psychologist told me this strategy works as it takes your attention off the memory and trigger.

∞∞∞∞

'Resilience is knowing that you are the only one that has the power and the responsibility to pick yourself up.'—Mary Holloway

∞∞∞∞

Show up & be determined

Showing up and being determined are attitudes towards life. By showing up, commitments are kept—even if we don't feel like it. We get up, dress neatly, arrive at appointments and work on time, are present mentally, organised and have a good attitude.

Showing up can be seriously difficult when you're stressed, have anxiety or depression or another mental illness, or are sick. I know this personally. When my anxiety and depression were severe, there were days when I desperately tried to show up to work or social occasions, but my mind and body wouldn't let me. Some days I stayed in bed.

I think the most important message I want to convey is; if you've made a commitment to someone or an organisation, you try your hardest to show up. Obviously, if you're sick or your mental illness is severe, that isn't going to happen but you then show the courtesy to let those people know. Don't decide at the last minute that you can't be bothered to go. Whether it's a meeting, a party or a sausage sizzle, there are people most likely relying on you, who want you there or will miss you. Just because you decide you don't feel like going, had a big night out beforehand, didn't set the alarm or have another weak excuse, if you have committed, then you go.

People I can think of who've been determined are J K Rowling, Susan Boyle and Jim Carey. Did you know that J K Rowling sent her manuscript for Harry Potter to around seventeen publishers and was rejected by all until eventually one small publisher accepted it, only printing 1,000 copies? Once her book won several prizes, it took off.

Scottish singer Susan Doyle's appearance led to the Britain's Got Talent judges being sceptical of her ability. Susan belted out the song I Dreamed a Dream. Her debut album was the UK's best-selling album of the year.

Jim Carey was booed off the stage the first time he did a stand-up comic act. When he auditioned for Saturday Night Live, he failed to land the part. Over time, he became known for his slapstick performances.

These people encountered rejection on multiple occasions. But did they let these rejections or setbacks stop them from pursuing their dreams? No. Why not? I believe they forged on because they felt they were good enough and they weren't prepared to give up on their dreams. They had self-belief, determination and resilience.

∞∞∞∞∞

'Success consists of going from failure to failure without loss of enthusiasm.'—Winston Churchill

∞∞∞∞∞

My mother has told me on numerous occasions that I was a determined youngster and teen. If I really wanted something, I went after it. My face, my social anxiety and my low self-esteem didn't stop me. That's something I continue to remember through life's setbacks and knockbacks.

To put it simply, determination can help you to stay motivated, be resilient and continue striving forwards and to lead your best life.

Twenty seconds of courage

Twenty seconds of courage is another self-taught strategy. It's useful for situations where you need to be assertive but are shaking in your boots.

I first used this strategy in 2014 to terminate the employment of a tutor. I was the coordinator of a community education program and a tutor had been causing issues for a long time.

Now, I had never fired anyone before and I hated conflict. I knew this wasn't going to be easy but I had to do it—so I held the phone and dialled the number. My husband and eldest daughter stood near me for support.

The rule of 'twenty seconds of courage' is pretty basic—you must do the hard action within twenty seconds. In this instance, it was to dial the tutor's phone number and not hang up.

With trembling hands, a pounding heart and shallow breathing, I picked up the phone and dialled. The phone rang and rang. I waited. Though inside me I wished she hadn't, the tutor answered and, with blood draining from my face, I delivered my message. She responded angrily to my news. I stood strong and firm. I told myself I had a job to do. After hanging up, my hands still shook but I was so proud of myself—I had done it!

Courage is acting anyway even though you feel fear.

Have hope

You can't change the past but you can look forward to the future and where you are headed.

To lead your best life, it's vital to accept the ups and downs of life. The metaphor, life is a rollercoaster, you just have to ride it, is true.

∞∞∞∞

'For I know the plans I have for you,' declares the Lord, 'plans to prosper you and not to harm you, plans to give you a hope and a future.'—Jeremiah 29:11

∞∞∞∞

So, what is hope? The dictionary definition of hope is *a feeling of expectation and desire for a particular thing to happen. It is also a feeling of trust.*

When you're being resilient, hope helps you acknowledge the bright side of life. It helps you discover opportunity in challenges and adversity rather than challenges in opportunities.

Hope allows you to see the possible good in the future.

Research has found that higher levels of hope counteract the negative effects of depression. Hope brings optimism for the future.

∞∞∞∞

Desmond Tutu once said, 'Hope is being able to see that there is light, despite all of the darkness.'

'We must accept finite disappointment, but never lose infinite hope.' —Martin Luther King Jr.

∞∞∞∞

Hope isn't a wish. The difference between hope and a wish is that the hopeful person isn't yearning for something positive to happen or to avoid danger or a challenge. No, the hopeful person is expecting and trusting that the thing they hope for will happen.

Research called Hope Theory states that hope gives the person the motivation to make positive choices and to take positive actions. These, in turn, will move a person along the path to success.

Research suggests there are also other benefits of having hope. These are that hope:

- helps support good mental health, reduces stress and anxiety
- helps to increase your self-esteem
- helps create and maintain happiness
- helps you to control your emotions
- improves your general health and immunity
- improves social relationships
- helps create and maintain an inner motivation to achieve

I make hope hearts out of clay and included with the heart is a card which reads, 'This hope heart is for you because with hope, one can think, one can dream and one can live.'

∞∞∞∞

In this chapter, I focused on resilience and explained why it's beneficial and will help you to lead your best life. In particular, I looked at making meaning from an event, coping with change, being a problem-solver, taking risks, learning from negative experiences and failure, having effective coping strategies, using the strategy 'Twenty seconds of courage' and having hope.

The next chapter, Chapter 7, contains my final thoughts on being weirdly wonderful, embracing our differences and leading our best life.

Chapter 7 - *My Final Thoughts*

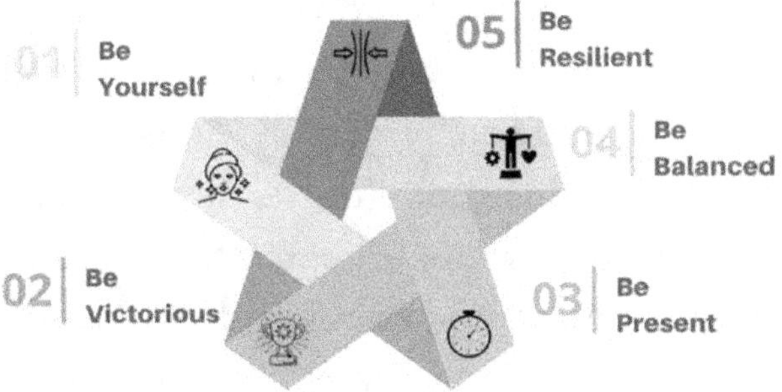

Thank you for making it to the end of my book! I really appreciate you journeying with me through these chapters and sharing in my stories. I hope I've helped you in some way to be leading your best life as a weirdly wonderful person.

I'd like to finish by summarising the key messages from each chapter:

Be Weirdly Wonderfully Yourself

To be leading your best life, you must own who you are—the imperfectly perfect and weirdly wonderful you. Taking off the fake mask and allowing yourself to be seen as flawed and different may be hard but, ultimately, it will have personal rewards. When you truly don't care what others think of you and you find your tribe who accept you for you, your confidence and self-esteem will thrive and blossom.

The world may try and beat you down and tell you that you don't belong—but that's a big, fat lie. You must ignore it. Go out there, be proud of who you are and be your true self.

Be Weirdly Wonderfully Victorious

To be leading your best life, you can't go around with your head down, hiding in the shadows or stuck in bad relationships. You must be living victoriously with goals and dreams and visions for your future. It's so important that you're able to recognise toxic relationships, prejudice and discrimination. And you can stand up for yourself by setting healthy boundaries. Knowledge is your power and you are worthy of respect.

Be Weirdly Wonderfully Present

To be leading your best life, you must aim to be in the moment as much as possible. Being in the moment means you're experiencing what's happening right now. Being in the moment means you're not worrying about the future or getting lost in the past.

Focusing on the present has many benefits—from enjoying what you're doing to staving off the limiting and negative thoughts that like to intrude and knock you down.

What's the most important time of day? NOW!

Be Weirdly Wonderfully Balanced

To be leading your best life, you must be looking after all aspects of your life—your social, physical, mental, spiritual, financial, career and family well-being. If one of these gets out of kilter, which is easily done, then the others will be affected. The objective of keeping in balance is to take care of yourself so you don't wear yourself out. May good health and happiness follow you all the days of your life!

Be Weirdly Wonderfully Resilient

And finally, to be leading your best life, you must be able to bounce forward when life's obstacles get in the way. As you well know, life is uncertain. There are always situations arising which you must swerve around, jump over or get back up from. Life really is a rollercoaster. Having resilience enables you to keep on going. It's that inner voice that says, 'You can do it. You've got this.'

∞∞∞∞

At the beginning of my book, I introduced you to the googly-eyed kid who was constantly being stared at, pointed at and bullied. I then shared with you her story, which is my story. As I said, I've had no dramatic turning point in my life that sent me in a completely different direction. My life has just been a hard slog. It's been a life of feeling like an alien and a misfit. To cope with all the good and bad in my life, I've developed certain mindsets and strategies. Many of these I learnt from my time spent with psychologists and others from my own personal reading.

I wrote this book to help others who feel the way I do. If you have a difference or a disability and you've had to fight to feel worthy of being on this Earth then I hear you. I stand with you. I believe in you. I refute the negativity that others have said about you and to you.

I've shared many stories about myself which illustrate why I chose my five 'be weirdly wonderful' strategies. Many of my stories are of hardship—but I must emphasise that it hasn't all been thorny. There's been plenty of gorgeous-smelling old-world roses in my life as well!

Psychological help, resilience, a sense of purpose and my faith have kept me going. I know that, when the chips are down, I can be determined, strong and courageous. I pray that, when your chips are down, you can too!

You've now reached the end of Be Weirdly Wonderful! Embrace your differences. What is one thing from my book that you can start implementing today? Or have you already put something into effect? I'd love to hear what the change in your life is or how my book has helped you. Please email me at jenny@jennywoolsey.com. I genuinely want you to be leading your best life!

I will finish with my saying:

You are good enough – in fact you are more than that—you are perfect the way you are!
Remember, no matter what you look like or feel like,
you are valuable and can achieve great things in life.

With love from me, Jenny

Bibliography

Ashfield, J. (2010) *Taking care of yourself and your family.* Australia: Peacock Publications.

Australian Government Department of Health and Aged Care (2021) *For adults (18 to 64 years).* Available at: https://www.health.gov.au/topics/physical-activity-and-exercise/physical-activity-and-exercise-guidelines-for-all-australians/for-adults-18-to-64-years

Australian Institute of Health and Welfare (2021) *Social isolation and loneliness.* Available at: https://www.aihw.gov.au/reports/australias-welfare/social-isolation-and-loneliness-covid-pandemic

Australian Institute of Health and Welfare (2022) *Family, domestic and sexual violence data in Australia.* Available at: https://www.aihw.gov.au/reports/domestic-violence/family-domestic-sexual-violence-data/contents/about

Beyond Blue (2022) *Learn about mental health.* Available at: https://www.beyondblue.org.au/mental-health#:~:text=The%20facts.%20In%20Australia%2C%20it%27s%20estimated%20that%2045,have%20depression%2C%20and%20over%202%20million%20have%20anxiety.

Beyond Blue (2022) *Signs and symptoms of anxiety.* Available at: https://www.beyondblue.org.au/the-facts/anxiety/signs-and-symptoms?&gclid=CjwKCAjwkrrbBRB9EiwAhlN8_Kl8bmMrv0-_pepx2RqE2weuu2gtLyg2yD9PJDQsMlhsANILZ7edrhoCnL4QAvD_BwE

Brook, B. (2017) '*They called me an idiot and said I should abort': The anguish of prenatal diagnosis.* Available at:

https://www.news.com.au/lifestyle/health/they-called-me-an-idiot-and-said-i-should-abort-the-anguish-of-a-prenatal-diagnosis/news-story/3ec2066d1696ce78b96c1470a8d0b2e9

Cleveland Clinic. (2024) *Sleep Apnea.* Available at:
https://my.clevelandclinic.org/health/diseases/8718-sleep-apnea

Cooper, O. (2012) *Psychological boundaries: What are psychological boundaries?* Available at:
https://www.transformationalwriting.co.uk/blog/psychological-boundaries-what-are-psychological-boundaries

Crenshaw, D. (2023) *Switchtasking verses multitasking. What is the difference?* Available at:
https://davecrenshaw.com/switchtasking-versus-multitasking-what-is-the-difference/#:~:text=But%20when%20most%20people%20try%20to%20multitask%20what,to%20move%20from%20one%20task%20to%20the%20other.

David, S. (2018) *How to build your resilience with Susan David.* Available at:
https://www.youtube.com/watch?v=oNqut813pas

Duggal, D., Sacks-Zimmerman, A. and Liberta T. (2016) *The Impact of Hope and Resilience on Multiple Factors in Neurosurgical Patients.* Available at:
https://www.ncbi.nlm.nih.gov/pmc/articles/PMC5120968/

Eisenmenger, A. (2019) *Ableism 101.* Available at:
https://www.accessliving.org/newsroom/blog/ableism-101/

Eldadah, B. and Nielsen, L. (2020) *Research on resilience in stressful times.* Available at:
https://www.nia.nih.gov/research/blog/2020/05/research-resilience-stressful-times

Fair Work Commission (2023) *Discrimination*. Available at:
https://www.fwc.gov.au/issues-we-help/discrimination

Finnerty-Myers, K. (2018) *A Scholar breaks down the real reasons we compare on social media*. Available at:
https://darlingmagazine.org/scholar-breaks-real-reasons-compare-social-media/

Ginsburg, K.R. and Jablow, M.M. *(2011) Building resilience in children and teens: Giving kids roots and wings.* 2nd ed. Elk Grove Village, IL: American Academy of Pediatrics

Glowiak, M. (2020) *What is self-care and why is it important for you?* Available at:
https://snhu.edu/about-us/newsroom/health/what-is-self-care

GoodTherapy (2018) *Overcoming prejudice.* Available at:
https://www.goodtherapy.org/learn-about-therapy/issues/prejudice-discrimination/overcome

Healthdirect (2020) *Work-life balance.* Available at:
https://www.healthdirect.gov.au/work-life-balance#:~:text=8%20tips%20for%20better%20work-life%20balance%201%201.,health%20...%208%208.%20Have%20down%20time%20

Healthdirect (2021) *Drinking water and your health.* Available at:
https://www.healthdirect.gov.au/drinking-water-and-your-health

Healthdirect (2021) *Mental health treatment plan.* Available at:
https://www.healthdirect.gov.au/mental-health-care-plan

Inge, C. (2022) *How to make a vision board that actually works.* Available at:

https://christieinge.com/9-steps-for-creating-a-vision-board-that-actually-works/

Interchange WA. (2024) *Duty of care and Dignity of Risk – What does it mean?* Available at:
https://www.interchangewa.org.au/blog/duty-of-care-and-dignity-of-risk-what-does-it-mean/

Johnston Chandler, D. and Johnston, C. (2023) *Cooling down teen stress*. Australia: Signs Publishing

Kanaat, R. (2016) *12 Famous people who failed before succeeding*. Available at:
https://www.wanderlustworker.com/12-famous-people-who-failed-before-succeeding/

Kavountzis, K. (2022) *8 reasons why self-care is important.* Available at:
https://www.beachbodyondemand.com/blog/why-is-self-care-important

Koydemir, S. (2020) *How to be resilient*. Available at:
https://psyche.co/guides/resilience-is-like-a-muscle-build-it-up-when-life-pulls-down

Mayo Clinic (2023) *Central sleep apnea.* Available at:
https://www.mayoclinic.org/diseases-conditions/central-sleep-apnea/symptoms-causes/syc-20352109

Mind Tools (2022) *Developing resilience.* Available at:
https://www.mindtools.com/ao310a2/developing-resilience

Mowbray, D. (2011) *Resilience and strengthening resilience in individuals.* Available at:
http://www.mas.org.uk/uploads/articles/Resilience_and_strengthening_resilience_in_individuals.pdf

Nash, J. (2018) *How to set healthy boundaries & build positive relationships.* Available at:
https://positivepsychology.com/great-self-care-setting-healthy-boundaries/

Nutrition Australia (2021) *Australian dietary guidelines: recommended daily intakes.* Available at:
https://nutritionaustralia.org/fact-sheets/adgs-recommended-daily-intakes/#Adults

Pawlowski, A. (2017) *How to worry better.* Available at:
https://www.nbcnews.com/better/pop-culture/praise-worry-why-fretting-can-be-good-you-ncna757016

Persaud, R. (2013) *Does fame make you more suicidal?* Available at:
https://www.huffingtonpost.co.uk/dr-raj-persaud/stephen-fry-attempted-suicide_b_3395012.html?guccounter=1&guce_referrer_us=aHR0cHM6Ly93d3cuZ29vZ2xlLmNvbS8&guce_referrer_cs=wTHlh4W7p47QNlKClLzzpA

Queensland Courts (2019) *What is domestic violence?* Available at:
https://www.courts.qld.gov.au/going-to-court/domestic-violence/what-is-domestic-violence

Raypole, C. (2019) *What makes a relationship healthy?* Available at:
https://www.healthline.com/health/healthy-relationship#quiz

Raypole, C. (2022) *What ableism means and why it matters.* Available at:
https://www.healthline.com/health/what-is-ableism#examples

Reachout (2022) *Mindfulness – is it for you?* Available at:
https://au.reachout.com/articles/how-to-practise-mindfulnes

Robinson, J. (2011) *Does pursuing our passions really make us happier?* Available at:
https://www.huffingtonpost.com/joe-robinson/pursuing-passions-happiness_b_812881.html

Sauber Millacci, T. (2017) *What is gratitude and why is it so important?* Available at:
https://positivepsychologyprogram.com/gratitude-appreciation/

SBS News (2023) *Why Australians are stressed more than ever.* Available at:
https://www.sbs.com.au/news/why-australians-are-more-stressed-than-ever

Schwantes, M. (2018) *Science says only 8 percent of people actually achieve their goals. Here are 7 things they do differently.* Available at:
https://www.inc.com/marcel-schwantes/science-says-only-8-percent-of-people-actually-achieve-their-goals-here-are-7-things-they-do-differently.html

Scott, E. (2023). *5 self-care practices for every area of your life.* Available at:
https://www.verywellmind.com/self-care-strategies-overall-stress-reduction-3144729

Sorvino, C. (2017) *Why the $445 billion beauty industry is a gold mine for self-made women.* Available at:
https://www.forbes.com/sites/chloesorvino/2017/05/18/self-made-women-wealth-beauty-gold-mine/#61c0bffb)2a3a

Stinson, A. (2024) *What is box breathing?* Available at:
https://www.medicalnewstoday.com/articles/321805

Suni, E. (2023) *What to do when you can't sleep.* Available at:
https://www.sleepfoundation.org/insomnia/content/what-do-when-you-cant-sleep

The Self Help Alliance (2011) *Building better boundaries.* Available at: https://www.ualberta.ca/anesthesiology-pain-medicine/media-library/documents/workbookbuilding-better-boundariesfeb2011.pdf

The Treatment Specialist (2023) *Celebrities who died by suicide.* Available at: https://thetreatmentspecialist.com/celebrities-who-committed-suicide/

Tribe, L. (2020) *Feeling isolated? You're not alone. Here's why 1 in 4 of us is lonely.* Available at: https://www.abc.net.au/life/social-isolation-why-are-we-so-lonely/10493414

Vogel, E., Rose, J. and Roberts, L. (2014) *Social comparison, social media and self-esteem.* Available at: https://www.researchgate.net/publication/275507421_Social_comparison_social_media_and_self-esteem

Wilson, K. (2019) *The inside story.* Australia: Karen Wilson

Acknowledgements

I wish to thank my growing community of supporters who encourage me and give me great feedback on my writing.

I write to help others.

I am thankful to my family for giving me space to write. I am extremely thankful to my partner, Ken, who continually encourages me, helps me with words and does a wonderful job of editing my books.

Thanks goes to the team at Self-publishing Lab for their help with the cover design.

To finish, I give glory to God who has given me the ability to write, has been with me through all my ups and downs in life and who has sustained my life. If it wasn't for my faith in God, I would not still be on this planet.

About the Author

I am an author, speaker, potter, teacher and disability advocate on disability, difference and mental well-being. My motto is Be Weirdly Wonderful! Embrace your disability and differences. I possess a Master of Education (Honours), a Certificate IV in Youth Work, a Certificate IV in Training and Assessment and certifications in speaking, creative writing and life coaching.

I was born with a rare craniofacial syndrome called Crouzon syndrome, have low vision and I use a long cane. I live with anxiety and depression and my children have disabilities and differences.

Home is north of Brisbane in Queensland, Australia with my youngest child, two aloof cats and my cute, fluffy dog.

I started writing stories when I was little. As a teenager, poetry was my favourite genre. In 2014, I left the primary classroom after 25 years and decided it was time to begin writing again. In 2016, I published my debut novel *Ride High Pineapple* which was endorsed by the Children's Craniofacial Association in the USA.

Ride High Pineapple was followed by:
- Brockwell the Brave (2016)
- Land of Britannica (2017)
- Daniel Barker: By Power or Blight (2018)

- Daniel Barker: Journey to Egypt (2020)
- Amy and Phoenix (2019)
- Amy and Phoenix: Time to Shine (2022)
- Simon Sees (2022) – Endorsed by Guide Dogs Qld and Shortlisted for 2024 Forevability Awards. *Revised 2024*

Anthologies I have short stories in are:
- Mater's 100 Stories (2006)
- Redemption (2017)
- Like a Woman (2017)
- What an Adventure! (Honourable mention) (2019)
- From the Edge (2019)
- Allsorts (Sydney Hammond Memorial Short Story Competition Long listed) (2019)
- Change Makers vol 5: 21 Transformational stories from women making an impact on the lives of others (Amazon best seller 2020)
- 2020: Year of COVID-19: Stories of Lockdown vol. 1 (2021)
- Short Stories of Science and Space (2021)
- Once Upon a Whoops! (Amazon best seller 2021)
- The Labyrinth and other stories of life (2021)
- Starlit Realms: A Fantasy Anthology (2022)
- Meanwhile… Murder (2022)
- It's a Kind of Magic: Stories and Spells by Second Rate Sorcerers (Amazon best seller 2022)
- Bones and Blue Eyes and other stories of life (2022)
- Game On (2023)
- Hot Diggety Dog! Tails from the Bark Side (2023)
- Terracotta Travellers and other stories of life (2023)
- A Tree Full of Crows (2024)

- Charms of Love (2024)
- The Dinner (2024)
- Talking Trees and other stories of life (2024)

I write to help people, whether it be children, teens or adults. Difference has been my entire life and I've had to learn to be my true self and be content with my differences. I've had to face my fears, stand tall and be strong and courageous on many occasions.

For my readers:

You are good enough – in fact you are more than that – you are perfect the way you are!
Remember, no matter what you look like or feel like,
you are valuable and can achieve great things in life!

You can find me in many places:
Email: jenny@jennywoolsey.com

Website: http://jennywoolsey.com/

Blog: Jenny Woolsey – Be Weirdly Wonderful:

http://jennywoolsey.blogspot.com.au/

Facebook:

https://www.facebook.com/JennyWoolseyAuthor/

Instagram: jennywoolseyauthor

YouTube: https://www.youtube.com/user/jennyw67

Please leave a review on Amazon and Goodreads and tell others about my book. I'd love to help as many people as possible to feel great about themselves and Be Weirdly Wonderful!

www.ingramcontent.com/pod-product-compliance
Lightning Source LLC
Chambersburg PA
CBHW051050050726
47592CB00002B/463